Dedication

This book is dedicated to every experience that shaped me, every challenge that awakened me, and every soul who crossed my path to teach me something meaningful.

To those who have supported me unconditionally — thank you.
You know who you are.

Your presence, your belief, and your love have meant more than words can ever say.
I carry deep appreciation for each of you.

— Melanie

Within you lives a version of yourself who already knows the way—all you have to do is listen, trust, and rise.

Contents

Chapter 3: **Understanding the Higher Self**

Chapter 4: **Connecting and Manifesting from Your Higher Self**

How to connect with your Higher Self and manifest from that place of alignment. Includes the Higher Self and Lower Self challenge to integrate what you've learned and begin living it daily.

Chapter 1:
The Journey – Introduction

Sometimes it's not about becoming
anything new, but about remembering
who you've always been.

I didn't always know there was a Higher Self and a Lower Self. What I did know was that I felt stuck—stuck in patterns I couldn't seem to break, thoughts that tore me down, fears that held me back, and a constant feeling that something inside me wanted more, but didn't know how to get there.

I've faced my share of challenges—deep insecurities, self-worth struggles, emotional pain, and moments where life felt like it was working against me. Through it all, I was always searching for answers, always hoping there was something more. That's when I started to notice two versions of me showing up in different moments of life.

One version responded with calm, trust, clarity, and vision. It was peaceful. It saw the bigger picture. It chose love over fear. That's the version I began to call my Higher Self.

The other version reacted impulsively, based on fear, trauma, ego, and old beliefs. It didn't think clearly—it just felt heavy. That was the Lower Self.

I gave them names because I needed a way to identify which part of me was speaking. And the moment I started asking myself, *Is this my Higher Self responding, or my Lower Self reacting?*—everything changed. That one question gave me awareness. And awareness is power. When I recognized the difference between the two, I had a choice. I could either let the past, the pain, and the fear keep running my life—or I could respond with intention, step into my power, and become the version of myself that creates, attracts, and manifests.

And here's what I discovered: manifestation happens from the Higher Self. You can't manifest peace, love, abundance, or joy from fear, doubt, and chaos. The more I chose my Higher Self, the more my life transformed. I started thinking differently, feeling differently, and acting from a new place of trust. I manifested things I once thought were impossible—not because I forced them, but because I aligned with the version of me that already had them. This book is your guide to understanding these two parts of you: The Lower Self, which we'll go into in the next pages, is the voice that keeps you stuck. It whispers all the reasons why you can't. But the Higher Self—the version of you connected to the Creator, to truth, to infinite possibility—that's where your power lives.

And when you live from your Higher Self, life begins to meet you there.

Chapter 2:
Understanding the Lower Self

You cannot heal what you refuse to face. Awareness is the first step to freedom.

– Yung Pueblo

Before we dive into the specific traits, it's important to understand what the Lower Self truly is—because this part of you has likely been influencing your thoughts, emotions, actions, and reality for far longer than you realize.

The Lower Self isn't evil or bad. It's simply the version of you shaped by fear, pain, doubt, comparison, trauma, and unhealed experiences. It's the part that reacts instead of responds. The part that plays small, hides your light, clings to comfort, avoids discomfort, and believes the worst might happen. This is where your limiting beliefs live. This is where the same patterns repeat.

Most people live from their Lower Self without even realizing it. They make decisions based on fear and call it logic. They procrastinate and call it perfectionism. The Lower Self is subtle—but powerful. It's that quiet inner voice convincing you to settle, to delay your dreams, to doubt your worth, and to stay exactly where you are.

This chapter is where you'll meet the many traits of the Lower Self. As you read through them, you might begin to recognize parts of yourself—gently and honestly. Because the truth is, we all want to manifest. But manifestation isn't just about desiring something—it's about becoming the version of you who can receive it.

And the traits of the Lower Self? They're often the ones holding us back.

Awareness is everything. When you understand these traits, you'll start to notice them in your own life. That awareness creates choice. And once you can see which part of you is operating—your Higher Self or your

Lower Self—you gain the power to shift. That's where transformation begins. That's when you become who you're meant to be. And that's when manifestation starts to feel natural—whether it's love, success, peace, abundance, or healing.

As you turn the next few pages, be honest with yourself. There is no shame. No guilt. Just awareness. Just observation. Notice what resonates with you. Reflect on the patterns you carry.

Each trait will include insights, questions, and mantras to help you bring awareness to your Lower Self—so you can gently release what no longer serves you and rise into the energy of your Higher Self.

Let's meet the Lower Self now—so you can rise beyond it.

Lower Self Trait 1: Fear

Fear is one of the most dominant traits of the Lower Self. It often shows up quietly—disguised as hesitation, overthinking, procrastination, or playing it safe. And yet, it has the power to stop you from becoming everything you're meant to be.

Fear isn't inherently bad. It exists to protect you. It wants to keep you safe, avoid pain, and prevent rejection or failure. But when fear runs your life, it doesn't protect your dreams—it protects your limitations.

Fear originates in the past. It's born from old wounds, trauma, disappointments, and experiences where something didn't work out. The mind, trying to protect you, says: *Let's not go there again.* So it builds walls. But those walls don't just keep pain out—they keep growth, love, and abundance out too.

When you live from fear, you manifest from survival. You make decisions based on what you're afraid might happen, not based on the life you want to create. You stay in comfort zones that shrink you. You settle, self-sabotage, or delay your dreams under the illusion of being "realistic."

But facing fear—really facing it—is where your power begins.

Because every time you do something you're afraid of, you expand. You become stronger, wiser, and more certain of who you are. You realize that fear was never the enemy—it was the gatekeeper to your next level. The very thing you're afraid of often holds the breakthrough you're seeking.

Fear is normal. You don't have to wait for it to disappear. You just have to stop letting it lead. Your Higher Self doesn't avoid fear—it moves through it.

When you start facing your fears, you step into your highest self—and that's when you become truly powerful.

Fear – Manifestation Reminder

When you let fear lead, you block the flow.

Fear tells the universe you're not ready. But when you face what scares you —even while shaking—you align with power. You become magnetic, brave, and capable of receiving everything you desire. Miracles happen when you move despite the fear.

Reflection:

Where in my life is fear holding me back right now?

What would my Higher Self do instead of letting fear lead?

Mantra:

I choose courage over comfort, faith over fear, and my Higher Self over my hesitation.

Lower Self Trait 2: Victim Mentality

Victim mentality is the mindset that whispers:

Why does this always happen to me?
It's not my fault!
They did this to me.

It convinces you that you're powerless—like life is happening to you, not through you. But when you live in this state, you give your power away. You hand over the pen and let someone else write your story.

Victim mentality carries an incredibly low frequency. It pulls your energy down—emotionally, mentally, spiritually. And what happens when you're vibrating at that level? You attract more of the same. More disappointment. More lack. More chaos. It becomes a loop—and you're stuck in it, repeating the same lessons until you finally choose to rise. This energy gives nothing back. It drains, delays, and deceives you.

It's your ego in disguise—telling you that you're safe if you just stay small, stay stuck, and stay angry. But here's the truth: your soul didn't come here to suffer. It came here to awaken.

How It Shows Up:

- You look around and feel like everyone else has it easier.
- You avoid taking responsibility because it feels too heavy.
- You hold on to the pain, believing it protects you from getting hurt again—but really, it's holding you hostage.
- You replay the same old stories, hoping they somehow end differently —without you having to change.

In Love: You feel unloved or unchosen—like you're never someone's first priority. Instead of setting standards, you lower them. You stay in unhealthy dynamics, thinking, *This is the best I'll get,* not realizing your energy is what's calling these patterns in.

In Work: You feel invisible or undervalued. But you don't speak up or strive better—you just stay resentful. You believe life gave others the tools and left you behind. Meanwhile, your talents stay buried under your own disbelief.

In Life: You blame the world. Your parents. The system. Your past. But deep down, you know the truth: no matter what's happened to you, you have the power to decide what happens next.

The Shift: Become the Creator Again

The opposite of victim energy is ownership.

When you stop asking *Why is this happening to me?* and start asking *What is this trying to teach me?*—everything begins to shift.

You are not weak.
You are not unlucky.
You are not stuck.

You are just disconnected from the truth of who you are. Take your power back.

Walk like your Creator walks with you—because they do.

Ask for strength, ask for guidance, and move forward with certainty even when you can't see the full path.

You were never meant to sit in pain and call it protection. You are meant to rise—to create, to choose, to transform.

Victim mentality is the voice of your ego. But your soul? Your soul is ready to take the lead.

Victim Mentality – Manifestation Reminder

You can't manifest from victimhood—you manifest from power.

The moment you stop asking, *Why is this happening to me?* and start asking, *What is this teaching me?*—your entire vibration shifts. You become a co-creator, not a bystander. That's when the universe begins responding differently.

Reflection:

Where in your life are you blaming instead of taking your power back?

How would your life change if you believed you were responsible for your healing?

Mantra:

I am not a victim of my story—I am the author of my next chapter.

Lower Self Trait 3: Control Issues

Control is often seen as a way of securing our world—keeping things predictable and safe. But in reality, control is a reflection of fear. Fear that things won't go the way you want them to. Fear that if you let go, chaos will ensue. And so, you keep everything in your grasp, believing that if you manage every detail, you'll be able to dictate the outcome.

But this need for control doesn't just drain your energy; it also shuts down the possibility of growth and flow. **When you're trying to control everything, you block the magic.** You become a prisoner of perfectionism and rigid expectations.

For example:
In relationships, you might find yourself constantly checking up on your partner, texting them first all the time, or overthinking every interaction. Instead of allowing the natural flow of connection, you try to control how it unfolds—how often you meet, when to say something, and even how much you give. You become so focused on managing the relationship that you miss the opportunity to truly enjoy it.

In your career, the need for control can manifest as an obsession with outcomes. You're so fixated on hitting specific milestones—getting that promotion, receiving validation, ticking off your to-do list—that you miss the moments that matter. You're not open to opportunities that come in unexpected forms because you're too focused on sticking to your plan. You don't trust that the universe has its own timeline.

In day-to-day life, this need to control can turn every decision into a heavy one. You might find yourself constantly planning, checking your calendar, and overthinking. You may even feel guilty when you're not being productive.

The Shift: Trust Over Control

The only way out of this is to embrace trust. Trust that life doesn't need to be micromanaged to unfold in your favor. Trust that surrendering to the unknown isn't weak; it's wise. When you let go of the constant need to control every outcome, you open up a space for magic, synchronicity, and unexpected blessings. Instead of clinging to the need for knowing everything, trust that what's meant for you will find its way to you. Ask the Creator for guidance and strength to move forward with confidence, even when you can't see the full path. Sometimes, stepping into the unknown is the most courageous thing you can do. Trust the process, even when it's not as clear-cut as you'd like.

When you stop holding on so tightly, life can surprise you in the best ways. Let go of the expectation of control, and allow yourself to experience the freedom and joy that comes from trusting the flow of life.

Control Issues – Manifestation Reminder

Trying to control blocks divine timing.

When you force outcomes, you limit the magic. Surrender opens the door to timelines and blessings greater than you imagined. Trust the unknown—it often delivers what control cannot.

Reflection:

What am I trying to control right now out of fear or insecurity?

Where can I surrender and trust instead?

Mantra:

I release the need to control and trust the flow of life.

Lower Self Trait 4: Jealousy

Jealousy can sometimes feel like an unwelcome guest. It shows up when you least expect it, and its sting is sharp. It often begins as a quiet comparison—noticing someone else's success, beauty, or happiness, and then feeling a little smaller, a little less-than. It whispers in your ear that there's not enough to go around, and someone else's win means your loss.

But jealousy doesn't need to be a destructive force. At its core, jealousy is a mirror, reflecting the desires you haven't yet claimed for yourself. It shows you what you secretly want—what you might not even believe is possible for you. And instead of allowing it to fester into resentment, you can use that feeling as guidance.

Jealousy says:
That should be me.

But your Higher Self says:
If it's possible for them, it's possible for me too.

When you're stuck in jealousy, it's easy to spiral into self-doubt. You start to question your worth, your timeline, your progress. You think, *What am I doing wrong?* or *Why is it so easy for them?* But that's the voice of the Lower Self—the part of you that compares instead of believes, that doubts instead of desires.

How It Shows Up:

- You compare your journey to others and feel like you're behind.
- You celebrate others publicly but feel bitterness or envy privately.
- You scroll through social media and feel drained, not inspired.
- You judge people who have what you want.
- You feel stuck and resentful because it feels like your time will never come.

For example, when you see a friend or a colleague succeeding, your first instinct might be to feel a twinge of envy. Instead of letting that turn into bitterness or self-doubt, use that feeling to reflect on why their success triggered you. Ask yourself:

What do I admire in them? What part of their journey excites me?

When you reframe jealousy this way, it becomes fuel to ignite your own dreams.

Think about it: in love, when you see someone else's relationship thriving—the kind of bond you desire for yourself—do you shut it down with jealousy? Or do you choose to celebrate it, knowing that what you admire in others exists within you? This is an opportunity to recognize the love you're capable of attracting, not an excuse to shrink or feel unworthy.

In your career, maybe you feel a little jealous of a peer who just landed a big promotion or a role you've been eyeing. Instead of seeing it as a sign of failure for you, recognize that it's proof that what you want is possible. It's evidence that you can have it too. Instead of comparing yourself to them, ask yourself how you can level up and align your energy with that success.

Jealousy has a way of making us feel like we're behind or not enough. But it's a signal that something you desire is within reach. The Universe wouldn't show you something you couldn't have.

From Comparison to Creation

Instead of letting jealousy drag you down, use it. Let it remind you of your desires and goals. Understand that the things you envy in others are clues to what's possible for you—and that you have the power to make it It's not a sign of weakness or insecurity; it's a sign that you're connected to something deeper—something you've been called to create in your own life. So, the next time you feel jealousy rise up, take a deep breath. See it for what it is: an opportunity for reflection and growth. Let it spark motivation, rather than fear. Let it remind you of your own power to create the life you desire. No one else's success diminishes yours—in fact, it strengthens the possibility of your own success.

You are not behind. You are not less-than. You are on your own journey. What's meant for you is already on its way.

Jealousy – Manifestation Reminder

Jealousy signals lack. Gratitude invites abundance.

If you want to attract more, celebrate what others receive. Your blessings come faster when you believe there's more than enough for everyone—including you.

Reflection:

What does my jealousy reveal about what I desire but don't believe I can have?

Can I let someone else's success be proof of what's possible for me?

Mantra:

What I see in others is a mirror of what's possible for me.

Lower Self Trait 5: Seeking External Validation

This one's a silent trap—because it often looks like ambition, confidence, or drive. But beneath the surface, it's rooted in something much deeper: Fear that you're not enough unless someone else says you are. When you live from a place of external validation, your sense of self becomes dependent on other people's opinions, praise, and approval. You start measuring your worth by how others see you—how many compliments you receive, how many likes you get, or how often someone tells you that you're doing well. But here's the truth: **when your self-worth is external, your peace is never stable.** One compliment can make your day, but one criticism can shatter your entire confidence. Let's look at how this plays out.

You finally wear the outfit that makes you feel amazing—but halfway through the day, you start wondering if others think you look good too. You post something that matters to you—a thought, a photo, a project—and then you refresh the page waiting to see how many people liked it. If the response is great, you feel high. If it's quiet, you start questioning yourself. *Was it not good enough? Am I not interesting anymore?*

In your career, you might chase roles or achievements not because they fulfill you, but because they impress others. You're constantly performing—doing what you think you should do to be seen as successful. But inside, you feel disconnected from your purpose. Because you're not creating from alignment—you're creating for applause.

Even in friendships or family dynamics, this shows up as people-pleasing. You say yes when you want to say no. You go along with things just to keep the peace or to be liked. You're afraid to take up space as your true self, so you shrink into who you think others want you to be.

Validation Comes from Within

It's time to come home to you.

You are not here to be approved of. You are here to be authentic.

The truth is when you truly validate yourself—when you know your worth, your gifts, and your value—the outside world no longer defines you. You stop needing people to clap for you because you've already claimed yourself.

Instead of asking, *Would they like it?*
You ask, *Does this feel true for me?*

Instead of waiting to be chosen, you choose yourself. Every time you catch yourself needing validation, pause and breathe. Ask yourself:

Would I still do this if no one saw it? Would I still say this if no one clapped?

If the answer is yes—that's alignment. That's power. And when you operate from self-worth, the world feels it. You attract respect, not because you chase it, but because you embody it. So release the need to be liked, praised, or approved of. Your soul didn't come here to fit in—it came here to shine.

Seeking External Validation – Manifestation Reminder

When you seek validation from others, you disconnect from your true source of power.

Manifestation flows through self-certainty, not outside approval. The more you depend on others to tell you who you are, the further you drift from alignment. Abundance comes when your validation comes from within—and from the divine, not the crowd.

Reflection:

Where am I waiting for others to approve of me before I feel enough?

What would change if I gave myself full permission?

Mantra:

I validate myself. My worth is not up for debate.

Lower Self Trait 6: Negative Self-Talk

One of the most harmful patterns of the lower self is that cruel, relentless inner voice. It whispers all the ways you might fail, all the reasons you're not enough, and all the scenarios where everything could go wrong.
It sounds like:

What if they don't like me?
What if I mess it up again?
What if I'm not good enough?
What if I fail?
What if I get judged?
What if I lose everything?

This is the voice that lives in the shadows of your mind, always preparing you for the worst. You play out conversations that haven't even happened, arguments that may never come, and disasters that exist only in your imagination. It convinces you that thinking about it nonstop will help you prevent it—but really, it just traps you in fear. Let's say you're starting something new—a relationship, a business, a move, a dream. Your soul feels excited, but that voice kicks in:

What if it doesn't work?
What if I end up alone?
What if I lose money?
What if I embarrass myself?

You obsess over every detail. You overthink your texts. You analyze their tone. You prepare for rejection before it's even hinted at. You water down your ideas because you don't want to be "too much." And slowly, without realizing it, you sabotage your joy. You hold back. You shrink. You hesitate.

This is how your thoughts manifest your reality. Because when you think like that—you act like that. You show up with doubt, fear, and resistance, and life mirrors that energy back to you. It's not that you're cursed or unlucky—it's that you're mentally and energetically stuck in the wrong story. And then comes the heaviness. The shame. You feel bad about feeling bad. You get frustrated with yourself for not being more confident or strong. But how can you expect to feel free when you're living in a mental prison?

The Shift: Train Yourself to Rethink

This voice doesn't disappear on its own—you have to interrupt it. You have to train your mind the same way you'd train a muscle.

Start by catching the spiral in real time. When your thoughts start with *What if...*, pause. Ask yourself:

- Is this actually happening right now?
- Do I have proof this is true?
- Am I imagining the worst because I'm scared—or because it's real?
- What if something goes right?
- What if I'm more capable than I think?

Remember, your mind is designed to protect you—not necessarily to empower you. That's your job. And you empower yourself by choosing better thoughts. Even when it feels awkward. Even when it feels fake. Even when you don't fully believe them yet. You speak to yourself with love until the fear starts to soften.

You remind yourself:
I can handle whatever comes.

You say:
I don't need to have all the answers right now, and I trust that life is unfolding for me, not against me.

The more you do this, the quieter the lower self becomes. Not because the fears disappear, but because you stop giving them power.

You are not your fears. You are not your worst-case scenarios. You are the creator—and your words are your tools.

Your thoughts are seeds. Plant what you want to grow. And when you feel yourself spiraling—overthinking, doubting, speaking down to yourself—here's one simple question that can shift everything:

What thoughts would the Creator have about this? How would the Creator handle this situation? How would the Creator show up in this moment? Let that sink in. The Creator wouldn't panic. The Creator wouldn't judge. The Creator wouldn't shame, doubt, or overthink. The Creator would trust. The Creator would love. The Creator would act with certainty, calm, and grace. So why not choose the same?

This single question reconnects you to your Higher Self—to the truth that you're not alone, you're not powerless, and you're not lost. You're just being invited to return to the light, one thought at a time.

Negative Self-Talk – Manifestation Reminder

What you say to yourself becomes your reality.

If you constantly feed your mind with doubt, fear, or shame, your outer world will reflect it. Speak to yourself like someone who is already becoming. Choose thoughts that match the life you're calling in.

Reflection:

Would I speak to someone I love the way I speak to myself?

What loving truth do I need to hear today?

Mantra:

I speak to myself with love, because I am worthy of love.

Lower Self Trait 7: Avoiding Important Things

Avoidance is that quiet behavior that feels harmless in the moment—until it starts ruling your life. It begins with small things:

You delay a tough conversation.
You push away a decision.

You ignore the uncomfortable emotion that's been bubbling under the surface. And slowly, you become an expert at pretending everything is fine—when deep down, you're overwhelmed, disconnected, and stuck. Avoidance isn't just about putting things off—it's about running. Running from pain. From responsibility. From truth. From transformation.

And as long as you run, you give fear the driver's seat. In love, avoidance can look like saying *it's okay* when it's really not. You don't speak up when you feel disrespected. You bottle things up, thinking silence is safer than confrontation. But all that suppression starts leaking out as resentment, confusion, or emotional distance.

In your personal goals, it shows up as unfinished projects and dreams that stay in your head, not your hands. You want to write the book, start the brand, apply for the opportunity—but you keep finding reasons to delay. Not because you're not capable, but because deep down, you're afraid of what might change if you actually follow through.

And when it comes to self-growth, avoidance is the habit of *I'll do the inner work later.* You distract yourself with everything external—staying busy, scrolling endlessly, or over-planning—instead of sitting with your feelings and asking, *What am I actually avoiding right now?*

The Shift: Face What You're Avoiding

The things you avoid the most are usually the things that hold your breakthrough. Avoidance only makes the fear louder. But when you finally turn around and face what you've been running from—the truth, the task, the feeling, the change—you take your power back.

It doesn't need to be perfect or dramatic. You don't have to tackle everything at once—just start by being honest with yourself. You ask:
What am I avoiding right now?

And then, without shame, you take the smallest step toward it.
Make the call.
Have the conversation.
Cry it out.
Write it down.
Take action.

Because clarity lives on the other side of confrontation. And healing begins when you stop avoiding what hurts and start tending to it with courage. You were not given this life to run away from it. You were given it to rise, step by step, into your full strength.

And when you stop hiding—from yourself, from others, from your purpose—you unlock a version of you that's grounded, clear, and truly free.

Avoiding Important Things – Manifestation Reminder

Avoidance delays your breakthrough.

Every time you avoid what needs to be done, you delay the next version of you. Growth, clarity, and manifestation live on the other side of what you're resisting. Face it—and let it free you.

Reflection:

What truth or emotion am I avoiding, and why?

What would happen if I faced it with courage?

Mantra:

I no longer avoid—I face, feel, and free myself.

Lower Self Trait 8: Always Finding Excuses

The lower self is a master of excuses. It will keep you stuck in your comfort zone, convincing you that it's safer, easier, and better to stay where you are. The comfort zone isn't comfortable. It's just predictable. It's where you settle when you stop believing that more is possible for you.

Imagine this: you set the alarm to wake up early, but the lower self whispers, *Just five more minutes... the bed feels so warm. Tomorrow will be better.* You plan to go to the gym, but suddenly, the voice inside says, *We'll go tomorrow, it's fine.* You decide to eat healthy, but by the end of the day, you hear, *You worked hard today, just one dessert won't hurt. Start tomorrow.* That's the lower self in full swing—always making excuses to keep you comfortable. It doesn't want you to stretch, to grow, or to break free from the cycle of "tomorrow." It wants you to stay small, stay where it feels easy and familiar, and keep avoiding the discomfort of change.

The lower self will tell you to quit halfway through a task. You start a project, get halfway through, and then it starts: *It's too much. You're too tired. You can finish it tomorrow. You've done enough today.* It makes you feel like what you're doing is hard, unnecessary, or not worth it. And the more you listen to that voice, the more you stay stuck. And this doesn't just happen in tasks. It can show up in relationships, especially when you've just been through a breakup.

The lower self will try to pull you back into the familiar—even if it's unhealthy. It tells you, *You miss them. Just one more call. Just one more meeting. It'll be different this time.* You might have self-worth issues, and when faced with discomfort after the breakup, the lower self feeds you the excuse of going back to the past. It convinces you that the familiar feels easier, and in that moment, it seems like the comfortable choice. But nothing new can enter your life when you're clinging to what's old. You have to be disciplined enough to break the cycle. You have to say no. You have to have the strength to remind yourself why you ended things in the first place and tap into your higher self to see the bigger picture. Your future self will thank you for the boundaries you set now. The shift comes when you decide to choose discilpine over comfort. You must wake up and make the decision to take action—even when you don't feel like it. Even when the lower self is whispering, *Rest*, you must push forward. You must recognize the excuses for what they are: distractions from your higher self. The comfort zone might feel easier, but it won't take you where you want to go. It won't bring you the life you dream of. The lower self is going to keep making excuses. It will always tell you that *tomorrow* is the right time. It will tell you that what you're doing is too hard. It will tell you that the comfort zone feels better. Nothing new enters your life when you're clinging to the old. Wake up. Now is your time. It's time to be disciplined. It's time to do the things you're avoiding. Every time you listen to the lower self, you're holding yourself back from greatness. Challenge it. Get out of the comfort zone. Your dreams are waiting for you, and the only way to get to them is to take that first step—even if it's uncomfortable, even if it's hard.

You have the power to do it. You have to do it—no excuses. The future version of you is depending on the choices you make today. Stop waiting for the right moment because it doesn't exist. Step out of the comfort zone now, and watch everything change.

Always Finding Excuses – Manifestation Reminder

Excuses delay your destiny.

Every time you justify staying small, you block the growth and opportunities trying to reach you. Manifestation requires action, not avoidance. The universe responds when you show up—even if it's imperfect, even if it's scary. Progress begins where excuses end.

Reflection:

Where am I choosing comfort over purpose?

What would happen if I stopped making excuses?

Mantra:

Discomfort is temporary—growth is forever.

Lower Self Trait 9: Expecting the Worst to Happen

This is the part of you that's always bracing for something to go wrong. You overthink, overprepare, and hold back joy—because you're secretly scared it won't last. Even in your happiest moments, your mind drifts toward *What if it all falls apart?*

This trait is rooted in mistrust—mistrust in life, in the universe, in people, and most of all, in God. When you don't feel spiritually supported, it's easy to believe you're doing everything alone. That loneliness breeds fear. And fear creates stories—stories that say it's safer to expect the worst than to get hurt hoping for the best.

You tell yourself it's *being realistic*, but in truth, it's self-protection. Your lower self believes that if you prepare for disappointment, it will hurt less. But what actually happens?

You stay stuck in anxiety.
You miss out on joy.
You block the very blessings you've been asking for.

How It Shows Up:

- You assume people will leave or betray you, even if they haven't.
- You worry about things going wrong before they even begin.
- You can't fully enjoy good news—you're already imagining what could ruin it.
- You feel uneasy when life feels too good, as if you're waiting for "the catch."
- You repeat phrases like *Knowing my luck...or Something always happens.*

This isn't just a mental habit. It's a spiritual disconnection. When you're aligned with your Higher Self, you live in trust—trust in timing, protection, and divine order.

But your Lower Self operates from control, fear, and doubt.

The Shift: From Fear to Faith
Your Higher Self doesn't live in fear—it lives in faith.
Faith in the timing.
Faith in the lessons.
Faith in your worth.
And most importantly, **faith in something greater than you.**

To shift, you must actively rewire your inner dialogue.
Choose to believe that things can go right, just as easily as they can go wrong.

Remind yourself: **fear is not truth—it's just a shadow.**
And your job is to bring light to it.

Speak From Your Higher Self Instead:

I trust that I'm protected and guided in every situation.
Things are always working out for me, even when I can't see how.
Good things are happening to me, and I allow myself to enjoy them fully.
I am divinely supported and safe to hope, dream, and believe.
I don't need to expect pain to protect myself from it.
I expect peace—and I create it.

Expecting the Worst – Manifestation Reminder

When you expect the worst, you attract the worst.

The universe mirrors your belief. If you keep bracing for things to go wrong, you're aligning with fear—not faith. Shift your expectations, and you shift your results. Expect the best, and you'll be ready to receive it.

Reflection:

Why do I assume things will go wrong before they've even begun?

What would it feel like to expect the best instead?

Mantra:

I expect miracles, not missteps. I am aligned with what's good and true.

Lower Self Trait 10: Unhealed Childhood Trauma

Your past is not your fault, but your healing is your responsibility.

Childhood is meant to be a time of safety, love, and wonder.
But for some people, it was a season of survival.

It was not a good experience—it was filled with confusion, fear, neglect, or emotional pain. Maybe you were raised in a home where money was always tight and your parents constantly stressed about it. Maybe you grew up hearing things like, *Only lucky people get rich*, or *People like us will never have that kind of life*. Without realizing it, you absorbed these beliefs as facts, and now, as an adult, you carry them like invisible weights in your mind.

Or maybe the trauma was deeper.
Perhaps you experienced abandonment, emotional neglect, or even abuse from someone who was supposed to protect you. You might have witnessed dishonesty between your parents and internalized it as truth—*Relationships aren't safe*, or *Love means betrayal.* You might have been told to stay quiet, to be good, to not cause trouble—and now, that silence has followed you into adulthood. You don't speak up for yourself. You tolerate what hurts you. You tell yourself this is normal, because it's all you've ever known.

These early wounds don't just fade with time.

When they go unhealed, they root themselves deep into your subconscious. They shape the thoughts you think, the people you attract, and the way you show up in life. You might chase partners who mistreat you because, deep down, you don't believe you deserve better. You might sabotage your own success because you're scared to outgrow the version of yourself that your childhood environment taught you to be. You might cling to relationships even when they're unhealthy, because being abandoned now feels like reliving the abandonment you felt then.

These traumas often create deeply embedded beliefs like:

- *I'm not lovable.*
- *I have to earn love by proving myself.*
- *Good things don't last.*
- *I can't trust anyone.*
- *If I speak up, I'll be punished.*

And the most dangerous part?
Most of these beliefs operate in the background of your life—unnoticed but incredibly powerful. They guide your choices. They influence how you see yourself. They make you doubt your worth.

Healing isn't about blaming your parents or reliving painful memories.
It's about understanding how those experiences shaped you so you can unshape them. It's about realizing that the beliefs you formed back then were built in survival—but they don't serve you now. As long as you allow those childhood wounds to run the show, you'll keep repeating the same painful patterns.

If you've ever wondered why you keep ending up in the same type of relationship, the same job struggles, the same emotional cycles—this might be why. Because a wounded child is still making your adult decisions.

It's time to take your power back.
You didn't choose what happened to you.
But you get to choose what happens next. And that starts with becoming

radically honest with yourself:

- What pain from your childhood are you still carrying?
- What limiting beliefs did you inherit that are not yours to hold?
- What behaviors do you justify simply because they feel "normal?

Normal isn't always healthy.
Familiar doesn't mean right.
And your past doesn't get to decide your future—you do.

Healing begins with acknowledgment. Then, with compassion. Then, with choosing a different path. That could look like therapy. Journaling. Inner child work. Or simply learning to speak to yourself kindly for the first time in your life.

Your wounds are not your identity.
They're chapters in your story—but they are not the whole book.

It's okay to grieve what you didn't get. But it's also your job to give yourself now what you never received then: love, validation, safety, belief.
That's what healing looks like.

And when you begin to heal those deep-rooted traumas, everything starts to shift:
Your relationships get healthier.
Your self-worth begins to rise.
You stop tolerating what doesn't feel good.
You realize you were never broken—just hurt. And hurt can heal.

Let this be the moment you stop blaming your past and start building building your future.
Because the version of you that is free from those childhood wounds?
That's your Higher Self. And it's waiting for you to come home.

Unhealed Childhood Trauma – Manifestation Reminder
What isn't healed can block what is meant for you.
Your childhood wounds may live silently in your energy and delay your manifestations. Healing allows you to feel safe enough to receive. Give your inner child the love and stability it never had—and watch your life expand.

Reflection
What experiences from my childhood still live in my body, my thoughts, or my choices today?
Where am I still repeating the pain I never got to process?
What would it look like to give myself now what I never received then—love, safety, or permission to speak my truth

Mantra
I am not defined by my past. I am worthy of love, safety, and joy. I release what was, and I choose what will be.

Lower Self Trait 11: Limiting Beliefs & the Absence of Abundance

The lower self doesn't just make you question your goals—it makes you question whether good things are even meant for you. It creates invisible walls in your mind: thoughts like *It's too late for me*, *Money is always a struggle*, or *Manifestation doesn't work for people like me*. These thoughts don't seem harmful at first—they can even feel like "realism"—but they quietly keep you stuck in a reality that doesn't reflect your potential. This shows up most painfully when you're in survival mode. Maybe you're drowning in debt or struggling with the pressure of constant financial instability. You might tell yourself you're being "practical" by accepting it as your reality—but every time you reinforce that belief, you keep your energy anchored in scarcity. **And energy creates reality.**

If you've ever hit rock bottom, you know how loud the lower self can get. It whispers that nothing will ever change. It uses your past to predict your future. It tricks you into believing that dreaming is dangerous because it might lead to disappointment. You stop praying for transformation and start praying just to escape the pain.

And while there's nothing wrong with seeking relief, healing happens when you ask for strength, perspective, and alignment—not just an exit. If you're consumed by fearful thoughts or anxiety about your future—or anything you're currently going through—begin by praying for certainty. Ask the Creator for guidance. Ask to be shown the way, to be given clarity, strength, and trust. Start a conversation that brings you back to your power. It doesn't have to be perfect—it just has to be honest.

From that space, you can start to gently rewrite the limiting beliefs that got you here. The lower self thrives on lack-based thinking, but when you become conscious of your beliefs, you reclaim your ability to shift them. The transformation starts when you allow yourself to see beyond the facts and into possibility. When you believe in abundance—even when you're sitting in lack—that's what creates the change: choosing to align your thoughts with what you want to experience, even when there's no sign of it yet. Not out of delusion—but out of knowing how powerful your beliefs are.

These limiting beliefs don't just delay your dreams—they shape your entire frequency. And your frequency calls in your reality. That's why you must become aware of them. Rebuilding your faith and retraining your thoughts is a daily practice—but it's the most powerful one you'll ever commit to.

Say to yourself:
Even now, I am shifting.
The universe is working for me, even if I can't see it yet.
My situation isn't my identity—it's just a chapter.

And when your mind spirals into fear or doubt, ask yourself this:

What would the Creator believe about this?
How would the Creator see this moment?
How would the Creator respond?

This one shift in perspective can bring instant clarity and peace. You stop reacting from fear and start choosing from trust. And that's where real manifestation begins.

Limiting Beliefs & Absence of Abundance – Manifestation Reminder

The universe has no limits—your mind does.

When you let go of the belief that things are impossible, your entire field opens. Shift into possibility. What you believe, you invite. What you expect, you attract.

Reflection:

What story do I keep telling myself about why I can't have more?

Where did I learn that I must struggle to receive?

Mantra:

I am worthy of abundance, ease, and more than enough.

Lower Self Trait 12: Lack of Self-Love

As you've probably heard, *self-love* and *self-worth* are not new concepts—and you'll hear about them again in the Higher Self traits as well. That's because they're **deeply important.** A lack of self-love or self-worth doesn't just affect one part of your life—it shows up **everywhere.**

Lack of self-love doesn't always scream.
Sometimes, it whispers through your choices.

It's not always about feeling broken or sad—sometimes, it looks like quietly settling. You accept less than you deserve, again and again—not because you want to suffer, but because, deep down, you don't truly believe you're worth more.

You put everyone else first—not just out of kindness, but because you've learned to believe your needs don't matter as much. You tell yourself it's fine, but it never really is. You stay in situations that don't feel good—not because you don't want better, but because a part of you has been convinced you're unworthy of more.

In relationships, this trait can be heartbreaking. You tolerate poor treatment. You chase crumbs of affection, thinking it's a feast. You hold onto someone who doesn't choose you fully because you're afraid no one else will. You mistake inconsistency for passion. You mistake intensity for love. You stay with people who are emotionally unavailable, unkind, or simply not right for you—because you fear that "better" doesn't exist for someone like you. Or worse, you believe you don't deserve it.

You ignore the red flags. You shrink to fit into their world. You overextend, overgive, and overexplain, just to be seen, chosen, and kept. And when they finally leave or disappoint you, you blame yourself—not realizing that the relationship just mirrored what you believed about your worth.

The truth is, your choices reflect your beliefs. If you don't believe you're valuable, you'll keep choosing people and situations that confirm that belief.

In your work, this shows up as hesitation. You don't pitch the idea, ask for the raise, or speak up in the meeting. You water yourself down because you don't think your voice matters. You tell yourself, *Im not ready. I'm not good enough* yet. You stay small—safe—but suffocated. This trait doesn't just block love or success. It dims your entire light. When you don't believe you are enough, your energy becomes a cycle of proving yourself—rather than knowing you already are.

The Shift: Reclaiming Worth by How You Treat Yourself

Healing begins when you stop waiting for someone to tell you you're worthy—and start acting like it.

Do you speak to yourself with love?
Do you set boundaries that protect your peace?
Do you walk away from what dishonors your soul?
Do you rest when your body needs it?

Do you surround yourself with people who reflect your light—or ones who benefit from your dimness?

Because here's the truth:
Your self-worth sets the standard.

You don't attract what you want—you attract what you believe you deserve.

You are not here to be half-chosen. You are not here to be tolerated. You are not here to prove your worth. You are here to remember it.

Lack of Self-Love – Manifestation Reminder

You manifest at the level of your self-worth.

If you don't love yourself, you'll attract people, jobs, and experiences that mirror that lack. Become the version of you who knows her value—and everything around you will rise to meet her.

Reflection:

Where do I rely on others to prove I am lovable or enough?

What can I start doing to show myself love every day?

Mantra:

I am enough as I am. I am lovable as I am.

Lower Self Trait 13: Fear of Rejection
When you fear rejection, you reject yourself first.

The fear of rejection is one of the most limiting emotional patterns a person can carry—*not because it screams loudly, but because it silently shapes who you become.* Unlike general fear, which is often rooted in survival, the fear of rejection is rooted in *belonging.* It's the belief that being accepted by others is more important than being connected to yourself.

And so, you shape-shift.
You shrink.
You silence yourself—not because you have nothing to say, but because you're afraid of how your truth will be received.

You might be brilliant, passionate, and full of vision—but still, you play small. You hesitate to share your ideas, your work, your heart—because what if it's not good enough?
What if *you're* not good enough?

This fear doesn't always show up dramatically. Often, it's quiet and subtle:

- You agree with things you don't believe in, just to keep the peace.
- You become whoever the room needs you to be, even if it means losing parts of yourself.
- You stay in unfulfilling situations because you'd rather be accepted than be alone.
- You don't ask for what you need, because you've convinced yourself that needing too much will push people away.

And here's the hardest truth:
You begin to reject yourself before anyone else ever gets the chance.

Imagine someone dreaming of launching their own business, writing a book, or starting a podcast. They feel the calling—but instead of moving forward, their mind starts whispering:

What if people laugh?
What if no one listens?
What if I fail?

And so, the dream quietly dies—not because they weren't ready, but because they abandoned it out of fear that others might abandon them.

In relationships, it's even more painful. You hide your opinions, suppress your desires, avoid difficult conversations—all to keep the connection intact. But it's not real connection if the *real you* isn't present. Love becomes a performance, not an expression. You give, hoping to be loved in return—but only with parts of yourself that feel "safe" enough to be seen.

This is how rejection trauma works: it creates a loop of self-abandonment.

You betray your own needs to avoid being abandoned by someone else.

The Shift:
Rejection is not proof that you're unworthy—it's a redirection toward alignment. Not everyone will accept you, and that's okay. What matters is that *you* do. Your job is not to be liked by everyone. Your job is to be honest, aligned, and **free.**

Next time fear creeps in and tries to silence your truth, remind yourself:
I'd rather be rejected for who I truly am than accepted for who I'm pretending to

be.

That is real freedom. And from that place, everything in your life begins to change.

Fear of Rejection – Manifestation Reminder

Fear of rejection keeps you from the opportunities meant for you.

You can't receive what you're afraid to reach for. The more you try to protect yourself from rejection, the more you reject your own expansion.

Say yes—even if it's uncomfortable. Even a "no" is divine redirection.

Reflection

Where in my life am I holding back who I truly am to be accepted by others?

When was the first time I felt rejected, and how has that moment shaped my behavior?

What would change in my life if I stopped trying to be liked and started being real?

Mantra

I no longer reject myself to be accepted by others. I choose truth over performance. I am safe to be who I really am.

Lower Self Trait 14: Inability to Forgive

Holding onto pain feels like control. That's illusion. When someone hurts us deeply—betrays our trust, breaks our heart, leaves us without answers —we carry that pain around like armor. Forgiveness feels like letting them off the hook. But here's what we don't realize: we're the ones still bleeding from a wound they caused. The inability to forgive is like drinking poison and expecting them to suffer. It keeps you bound to the past, energetically and emotionally. This trait doesn't just affect your thoughts. It alters your energy.

When you carry resentment, even unconsciously, it becomes a vibration that influences every new experience. You start building walls instead of bridges. You keep people at a distance. You assume new situations will end the same way the old ones did. And you're not wrong—because that's exactly what you start to attract—the same patterns in different faces. Let's say you were betrayed by someone you trusted deeply. That betrayal planted a seed of distrust so strong that now, even when you meet someone genuine, your guard is always up. You overanalyze, doubt their intentions, and sabotage the connection before it can grow. Not because you don't want love—but because you haven't healed from what came before it.

In your career, it might look like avoiding leadership roles or new opportunities because someone once dismissed your ideas or made you feel small. You unconsciously believe that stepping up will only lead to more pain. So you stay where it feels familiar—even when it doesn't serve you anymore.

The Shift:

Forgiveness isn't about them. It's for you. It's choosing to stop carrying what isn't yours anymore. Emotionally, it creates space. Energetically, it opens portals to freedom. Forgiveness doesn't mean what happened was

okay—it means you're ready to move on without it defining you. Start by acknowledging how heavy the past still feels. Forgiveness doesn't mean you have to hang out with someone again.
It means you're clearing the energy between you and that person—for your own peace. You're letting go of the heaviness, the grudge, the emotional weight.

Everyone makes mistakes, and while some things may be unacceptable, forgiveness is still important—especially for you.

That thought of *this person did this to me* is not healed energy. It means the experience still holds power over you.

Yes, forgiveness takes time. But one day, you have to decide to free yourself—from the pain, the story, and the person.
And when you do, trust me—it will set you free.

Inability to Forgive – Manifestation Reminder

You can't manifest light while holding onto heavy energy.

Grudges, anger, and bitterness block joy. Forgiveness isn't approval—it's release. When you clear the emotional weight, you clear the path for what's truly aligned.

Reflection:

What pain am I still holding onto that's keeping me stuck?

Am I willing to free myself by releasing it?

Mantra:

I forgive to free my heart—not to justify the pain.

Lower Self Trait 15: Fear of Change

Change threatens everything the lower self clings to—control, safety, routine, familiarity. That's why it resists it so hard. But nothing new can enter your life when you're clinging to what's old.

The fear of change makes you stay in situations long after they've stopped serving you. You convince yourself, *At least I know what to expect here.* Whether it's a job you've outgrown, a city that drains you, or a version of yourself that no longer feels right—you stay, because the unknown feels scarier than the pain you already know.

Imagine living in a city where you constantly feel uninspired and stuck. You daydream about moving somewhere else, somewhere that feels alive and expansive. But every time the idea gets close, your mind spirals: *What if I don't find a good home? What if it doesn't work out? What if I regret leaving?* And so, you stay—not because your soul wants to, but because your fear won the argument.

Or think of someone staying in a job that drains them every single day. They complain about it, they dream of doing something more meaningful or starting their own business, but when the opportunity comes, the fear says, *What if the money doesn't come? What if I fail? What if I lose everything?*

Even in relationships—fear of change can trap people in toxic dynamics. You might know it's not love, not peace, not what your soul truly wants—but the idea of starting over, of being alone for a while, or of facing your patterns feels too overwhelming. So you tolerate what's familiar, even if it's slowly draining your spirit.

Sometimes, the fear is in the smaller shifts: moving into a new home, leaving a friend group that no longer aligns, choosing healthier habits that disrupt your current lifestyle, or even starting therapy. It's all change

—and it all requires courage.

In your personal growth, fear of change might sound like, *This is just how I am* when deep down you know it's just how you've been. The person you're becoming requires different choices. It requires new habits, new boundaries, new beliefs—and that can feel terrifying when your identity is attached to the old.

The Shift:

Change is the path to everything you've been asking for. You cannot manifest a new life while staying loyal to your old patterns. Yes, it will be uncomfortable. Yes, your mind will try to protect you by playing out every worst-case scenario. That's not intuition—that's fear dressed up as logic.

The universe responds to movement. Take one step, and you'll be shown the next. When you feel fear, pause and speak to the Creator. Ask, *Help me trust what I can't yet see.* You don't need to have it all figured out—you just need to be willing.

Remember: nothing changes until you do.

Fear of Change – Manifestation Reminder

Your next level requires a new version of you.

Change may feel uncomfortable, but it's the only way forward. If you're resisting change, you're resisting the very path that leads to what you've asked for. Let go of the old—you are safe to grow.

Reflection

What am I afraid will happen if I allow change into my life?

Is it really the change I fear—or is it the loss of control and certainty?

What part of me is holding on to comfort, even when it no longer feels aligned?

Mantra

I release the need to stay the same. I trust that change is guiding me closer to my truth. I am safe to evolve, grow, and expand.

Lower Self Trait 16: Lack of Boundaries

When you lack boundaries, you open the door to burnout, resentment, and constant exhaustion. Boundaries are essential for your well-being. They protect your energy, preserve your peace, and ensure that you don't lose yourself in the demands of others. But when you're living from your lower self, you struggle to create or maintain these boundaries. Instead, you say yes when you mean no, you overextend yourself, and you let people take more than they give.

The lower self convinces you that you have to please everyone. It tells you that if you say no, you'll be rejected. It tells you that if you don't give endlessly, you're selfish or unworthy. But the truth is: not setting boundaries isn't an act of love—it's an act of self-sabotage.

When you lack boundaries in relationships, you allow others to dictate your emotional state. You might constantly give without receiving, always putting their needs before your own. You let them take up all your mental space, always wondering if they're happy, if they're pleased with you, or if they need you to fix something. The result? You feel drained. You begin to lose yourself in the relationship, forgetting who you were before all of this. Maybe you're afraid of conflict, so you keep quiet when you're hurt. Or perhaps you're afraid of being alone, so you tolerate things that don't align with your values. Over time, this erodes your self-worth, and resentment builds up.

In your job, a lack of boundaries might look like saying yes to every task, even when you're already overwhelmed. You might feel the pressure to constantly prove your worth, working long hours, responding to emails at all hours of the night, and allowing work to take over your personal life.
Eventually, this leads to burnout. You feel unappreciated because you neglect your own needs for the sake of others, the more exhausted you become. And in the long run, it becomes harder to perform well because

you're not nourishing yourself—physically, mentally, or emotionally. Without boundaries, you let the world dictate how you feel. The news, social media, the people around you, their opinions, their needs, their problems—everything pulls at your energy, leaving you little to no space for your own desires.

You may find yourself caught up in drama that doesn't even concern you, feeling obligated to take on others' burdens, and spreading yourself thin in a million directions. And then you wonder why you feel so disconnected, overwhelmed, and out of touch with yourself. The lower self convinces you that you should be all things to all people, but that is a recipe for chaos, not fulfillment.

The Shift: Establishing Healthy Boundaries

Setting boundaries is one of the most loving things you can do for yourself. It's not about shutting people out—it's about allowing space for you to nurture and honor yourself. The first step is realizing that you are worthy of protection. Your time, your energy, your emotions—they are yours to manage.

Here's how you can start:

•Learn to Say No:

It's simple, but it's often one of the hardest things to do. When you feel yourself agreeing to something out of guilt, fear, or obligation, stop and ask yourself: *Is this in alignment with my highest good*? If the answer is no, kindly, but firmly, say no.

• Communicate Your Needs Clearly:

Boundaries aren't just about saying no; they're also about expressing what you do need. If you're constantly taking on tasks at work that you're not

responsible for, let your team know what your limits are. If a friend is emotionally draining you, explain
how you need space. Be clear, direct, and compassionate.

• Prioritize Yourself:
It's easy to get lost in everyone else's needs. But when you make your own well-being a priority, you show the universe that you value yourself. You fill your own cup first, and from that space, you can give to others with true love and intention.

• Set Emotional Boundaries:
This is about protecting your peace. Don't allow others to dump their emotional baggage on you. When someone is projecting their negativity, remind yourself: *That's not mine to carry.* You don't need to take responsibility for others' emotions, and you don't need to fix them.

• The Power of Boundaries in Your Life:
When you establish strong boundaries, you start to experience a deep sense of freedom. You will no longer feel drained, overwhelmed, or like you're constantly people-pleasing. Instead, you'll feel confident, empowered, and aligned with your true self. Boundaries are an expression of self-love—and by setting them, you are teaching others how to treat you with respect. Most importantly, you're teaching yourself to honor your own needs.

• A Simple Practice for Boundaries:
Every time you feel guilt or resistance about setting a boundary, pause and ask yourself: *Am I protecting my peace? Am I honoring my needs?*
If the answer is yes, stand firm in that boundary with love and confidence.

Lack of Boundaries – Manifestation Reminder

Without boundaries, your energy leaks into what doesn't serve you. Saying yes to everything tells the universe you don't know what you want. Boundaries are an act of self-respect—and clarity. The more you honor your energy, the more aligned your manifestations become.

Reflection:

Where am I saying "yes" when I want to say "no"?
What does it cost me when I don't protect my peace?

Mantra:

My boundaries honor my energy and protect my peace.

Lower Self Trait 17: Lack of Patience

Patience is something we often overlook, especially in a world that thrives on instant gratification. But the lack of patience—particularly when it comes to our dreams—is one of the most dangerous traps set by the lower self. When we're impatient, we expect results right away. We want things to happen on our timeline, not in divine timing. This leads to frustration, burnout, and sometimes even giving up on what we truly desire.

Impatience is often rooted in fear: the fear that things won't work out, that we'll be stuck forever, or that we're not worthy of having our dreams come true. It makes us doubt ourselves and the process. We rush. We push. We try to force outcomes instead of allowing the universe to align things in their perfect time.

This shows up in every area of life:

In Relationships

Impatience can make you rush into a relationship out of fear of being alone or left behind. After a breakup, you may feel a strong urge to "fill the void" quickly, even if it means settling for someone who doesn't align with your values. You might ignore red flags or rush intimacy, just to feel loved or accepted again.

It also appears when you compare your love life to others. If friends are getting married or entering long-term relationships, you might feel pressured, asking, *Why is it taking so long for me?* You start making decisions based on fear—fear of being behind—rather than waiting for the right connection that truly supports your growth.

Impatience in relationships can also manifest when you expect immediate change in yourself or your partner. You might think that just a few months of healing or effort should be enough. But transformation takes time.

Solution: Trust that love will meet you when you're ready to receive it. Don't rush the healing. Embrace this space as a sacred time to build your self-worth, so you can attract a partner who truly matches your energy.

In Health and Fitness

Impatience here leads to unrealistic expectations. You might expect your body to change within weeks and get frustrated when the scale doesn't move or visible results don't show. This frustration can cause you to quit, or swing to the other extreme—crash diets, overexercising, or punishing routines.

You may jump from one workout to another, one diet to the next, constantly searching for a quick fix. But sustainable change doesn't happen in a rush—it happens in consistency.

Solution: Focus on how you feel, not just how you look. Celebrate wins like better sleep, more energy, or improved confidence. Remember, your body is transforming even when the mirror doesn't show it yet.

In Career and Business

When you're building a dream, whether it's a brand, a project, or a career shift, impatience can be your downfall. If success doesn't come quickly, you might feel discouraged. You might want to abandon it altogether, thinking, *Maybe this isn't meant for me.*

But real growth takes time—learning the ropes, building a network, gaining trust, and refining your message. The behind-the-scenes work is never wasted.

Solution: Measure progress in small wins. Every post you publish, every person you impact, every mistake you learn from—it's all part of the journey. Keep showing up, even when results feel far away.

In Personal Growth
You start a journaling practice, meditation, or self-reflection. At first, you feel great. But after a few weeks, the excitement fades, and you wonder, *Why don't I feel better yet?* You expect your inner world to transform overnight, but healing doesn't follow your schedule.

True personal growth is often invisible at first. You may not notice the change day by day—but look back after a year and you'll see how far you've come.

Solution: Keep going. Be gentle with yourself. Let progress be messy and nonlinear. The work you're doing is making a difference, even if you can't see it yet.

The Shift: From Instant Gratification to Long-Term Fulfillment
Impatience is the lower self's way of telling you you're behind. But you're not. You're exactly where you're meant to be. Every delay is divine redirection. Every pause is protection.

Train your mind to celebrate *progress*, not perfection. Learn to love the *process*, not just the outcome. And most of all, trust that your dreams are not only possible—they are promised. But they'll arrive when you're truly ready to receive them.

When you are truly patient, you stop obsessing over the when and start focusing on the who.
Who are you becoming in the process?

Your Higher Self trusts that every delay is either a redirection, a preparation, or a protection.
Every *not yet* is still part of the plan.

Lack of Patience – Manifestation Reminder
Some things take time because you're still becoming.
Impatience creates pressure. But timing isn't punishment—it's preparation. What's meant for you is never late. Trust the process, and don't rush your becoming.

Reflection:
Where am I rushing the process because I don't trust the timing?
Can I enjoy who I'm becoming while I wait?

Mantra:
I trust divine timing. I am on my way, even when I can't see it.

Chapter 3:
The Higher Self

Your Higher Self already knows the way. The work is to get quiet enough to hear it.

– Melanie Singh

You've just met the voice of your Lower Self—the part of you that holds on to fear, doubt, and familiar patterns. But you are not meant to live from that place. You are meant to rise.

Now it's time to meet the other side: the version of you that already exists within—your Higher Self.

This isn't some fantasy version of you. It's real. It's powerful. It's the you that exists beneath the layers of conditioning, pain, and fear. And the more you choose alignment over avoidance, love over fear, and growth over comfort, the more this version begins to lead.

Your Higher Self is your inner guide. It's the quiet wisdom in the chaos. It's the version of you that believes deeply in abundance, purpose, joy, and possibility—even when the outside world tries to tell you otherwise.

And here's the beautiful truth: when you begin to recognize it, connect to it, and live through it, your life begins to change—not just on the outside, but from within. From your thoughts, your choices, your boundaries, your habits—everything shifts when you lead with your Higher Self.

This is the self that helps you manifest the life you dream of. This is the self that makes your vision real.

Now let's uncover the traits that define your Higher Self, so you can begin to embody this version of you more and more—not just someday, but every single day.

Higher Self Trait 1: Self-Awareness

Self-awareness is when you begin to observe your thoughts, beliefs, and actions—many of which you were previously unconscious of. Instead of reacting on autopilot, you start noticing your patterns without judgment, without immediate emotion, and without needing to fix or control anything right away.

You simply observe.
And that is where transformation begins.
Because when you stop reacting, you start responding.

You pause.
You reflect.
You choose aligned action.

It notices.
It pauses.
It reflects before it reacts.

It asks powerful questions like:

- *What am I truly feeling right now?*
- *Why did this trigger me?*
- *What belief, wound, or fear is this connected to?*

That moment of inquiry becomes a gateway.
Instead of repeating old patterns, you begin to heal them.

Self-Awareness Is a Daily Practice

It's not something you achieve once—it's something you cultivate every day.

It lives in the small choices:

- Catching yourself mid-spiral and choosing to breathe
- Pausing before responding to a triggering message
- Recognizing when you're numbing out instead of tuning in

Self-awareness helps you shift from reaction to response, from blind habit to conscious choice.
Without it, you repeat cycles.
With it, you begin rewriting them.

What It Sounds Like in Real Life
You feel hurt that someone didn't reply to your message.

Your Lower Self whispers:
They don't care. You're not important. This always happens.

But your Higher Self steps in and says:
Pause. Why does this feel so familiar? Is this really about them—or is this poking an old wound around rejection or being ignored?

Instead of spiraling, you get curious.
That one shift—**awareness**—saves you hours of emotional reactivity.

What Changes When You Live With Self-Awareness

- You catch your patterns before they control you.
- You recognize when your behavior is driven by fear rather than truth.
- You stop blaming others and start asking what the moment is here to teach you.
- You separate your intuition from your inner critic.
- You become more intentional with your actions, your words, and your energy.

- And perhaps most powerfully:
- You begin to meet yourself instead of abandoning yourself.

You begin to meet yourself instead of abandoning yourself.

The Result: Clarity, Empowerment, and Growth

The more self-aware you become, the more empowered you feel.
You stop walking in circles.
You begin walking in alignment.

You realize that you have the power to shift the way you experience life—not by controlling others, but by understanding yourself.

Self-awareness is the compass of your Higher Self.
It helps you realign in moments of chaos.
It helps you lead yourself when the world feels loud.
It turns confusion into clarity—and habits into healing.

Real-Life Examples of Self-Awareness in Action

- You feel jealous of a friend's success, and instead of judging yourself, you ask: *What does this show me about my own desires?*
- You start snapping at your partner and pause to ask: *Am I actually upset with them, or am I projecting my stress?*
- You cancel a plan—not out of avoidance, but because you're aware that your body needs rest, not distraction.
- You journal instead of scrolling, reflect instead of react, and ask *why*? before you assume.

Self-awareness isn't about overthinking.
It's about remembering.
Remembering that you are not your thoughts.
You are the one who watches them.
And from that place of awareness—
You can choose again.

Self-Awareness – Manifestation Reminder

Self-awareness is the key to transformation.

When you can observe your thoughts, patterns, and energy without judgment, you hold the power to shift them. You begin to catch what's misaligned and choose again. That's how you manifest—by becoming conscious of the energy you're sending out.

Reflection:

Where in my life am I reacting instead of responding?

What patterns keep repeating—and what might they be trying to show me?

Mantra:

I am not my thoughts. I am the one who observes them.
With awareness, I choose alignment over reaction.

Higher Self Trait 2: Practicing Self-Love

Self-love isn't a trend. It's a return to who you really are.

We've explored what a lack of self-love can do—how it shapes your choices, your relationships, and your sense of worth. Now, it's time to shift.

Not just to understand self-love—but to *practice* it.

Not as a concept, not as a buzzword, but as a way of *being*.

Self-love isn't makeup or a mask.

It's not external. It's a quiet revolution within.

It's when you stop waiting for permission to feel good about who you are.

It's when you finally say, *I am enough*, and truly mean it.

Your Higher Self is rooted in love—and that love begins with *you*.

You'll hear self-love echoed throughout the other traits too—because it's one of the most important energies you can carry.

Practicing it consistently will change your life.

Self-love is filling your own cup, not out of pride, but out of presence.

It's recognizing that your energy, your time, your body, your peace—are sacred.

You become more mindful of what you allow into your space.

You rest without guilt. You nourish your body.

You move to feel alive.

You speak to yourself with kindness instead of criticism.

Self-love is learning boundaries—not as walls, but as gates.

It's saying "no" without explaining. It's choosing your peace over people-pleasing.

It's knowing that protecting your energy is not selfish—*it's wise.*
It's no longer betraying yourself to belong.
It's choosing yourself when it would be easier to shrink.
It's believing in your own vision—even when no one else claps.
It's waking up with discipline—not out of pressure, but out of *respect for your dreams.*

You rise above excuses.
You stop negotiating with your lower self.
You build structure, routines, and rituals to serve your *future,* not your comfort zone.

And most importantly, self-love is *knowing your worth and living it.*
It's not just about feeling valuable.
It's about *acting like it, speaking like it, walking like it, charging like it.*
You don't wait for the world to recognize your value—you carry it.
Even if someone else can't see your light, that's their blindness—not your truth.

In relationships, self-love changes everything.
The moment it becomes non-negotiable, your relationships begin to shift.
You're no longer begging to be chosen—you've already chosen yourself.
You stop confusing chaos for love.
You crave peace over adrenaline.
You communicate clearly.
You don't settle for being "almost loved."

You walk away when your needs aren't met—not because you're cold, but because you know your warmth is sacred.
You no longer chase those who breadcrumb you, confuse you, or ignore you.
You know now that *peace is more attractive than pain that burns you.*

You attract partners who respect your standards—because you embody them. You recognize red flags faster because your inner world is no longer used to pain. You feel whole on your own, so love becomes a beautiful addition, not a crutch.

Whether you're single or in love—your world remains intact.

You bring your full self to the table.
And that's what makes you magnetic.

Because when you live in self-love, you're free:
Free from the opinions of others.
Free from the cycle of proving, pleasing, and performing.
You become grounded in your worth, disciplined in your dreams, gentle with your mind, and loving to your body.

You treat yourself like royalty—not because you're better than anyone, but because you finally see yourself clearly.

And the more you love yourself, the more you vibrate at the frequency of abundance.
That's where alignment lives.
That's where miracles meet you.

We'll explore more of this in the traits ahead—self-worth, presence—so you can truly understand it, live it, and *become it.*

Practicing Self-Love – Manifestation Reminder

The more you love yourself, the more the universe loves you back.

When you deeply care for yourself—your body, your mind, your time—you raise your standards. You stop settling, and start attracting people, opportunities, and outcomes that match your worth. Keep showing up for you. You are the foundation.

Reflection:

Where in my life am I still waiting for someone else to validate me instead of validating myself?

What would my day look like if I treated myself like someone I truly loved?

What boundaries, routines, or habits would support the version of me that fully loves and respects herself?

Mantra:

I am already enough. I honor my energy, my needs, and my worth. I don't shrink —I rise. I don't chase—I attract. I love myself, and that love shapes everything I do.

Higher Self Trait 3: Emotional Responsibility

Your Higher Self doesn't blame.
It doesn't project.
Instead, it takes full ownership of every emotion—without shame, avoidance, or denial.

When you're emotionally responsible, you no longer say,
They made me feel this way, or *It's because of them that I'm upset.*
Instead, you pause, reflect, and ask:

Why did that trigger me?
What part of me is still unhealed or reactive?

This doesn't mean you suppress your emotions or pretend to be unaffected.

Emotional responsibility is not about being numb—it's about being conscious.

It's recognizing your feelings as valid while also understanding that how you act on them is your choice.

Your Lower Self wants to react—yell, withdraw, guilt-trip, overthink, or play the victim.
It wants to spiral.
But your Higher Self pauses. It observes. It chooses peace over drama.
It chooses a higher response—not for them, but for *you.*

Taking responsibility for your emotional state is powerful because it gives you your power back.

When you stop handing your peace over to other people's actions, words, or moods, you become unshakable.
This is where real freedom begins.

You're no longer controlled by outside circumstances.
You respond from clarity instead of pain.
You become intentional in your words, your choices, and your presence.

Daily Practices for Emotional Responsibility

• Pause before reacting.
When something triggers you, take a deep breath and give yourself a moment to observe what's really going on within you before responding.
Ask yourself, *What part of me is feeling this way?*
Instead of blaming the other person, look inward.
Is it insecurity? Abandonment? Fear? Naming it gives you clarity.

• Journal your triggers.
Each time you feel emotionally activated, write it down and reflect.
What patterns do you see?
What beliefs are you carrying that are causing pain?

• Use "I" language.
Shift from *You made me feel...* to *I feel...* to take ownership of your emotions instead of projecting them.

• Take space when needed.
Being responsible doesn't mean reacting instantly.
Sometimes emotional maturity means walking away, calming down, and returning later with a clearer heart.

• Choose peace, not power.
Don't try to win—try to understand.

Emotional responsibility is about being centered, not controlling.

The more you take responsibility for your emotional world,
the more empowered, calm, and conscious you become.
This is your Higher Self in action.

Emotional Responsibility – Manifestation Reminder
You can't manifest from chaos—you manifest from clarity.
When you stop letting your emotions control your actions, you gain emotional intelligence—and emotional freedom. Feel your emotions, but don't become them. When you stay in peace, presence, and purpose, manifestation becomes effortless.

Personal Note:
This trait changed my life. I used to let emotions ruin my day. Now I acknowledge them, understand where they come from, and lead myself gently back into alignment. It's not about ignoring your feelings—it's about not letting them define you. This is where peace and power meet.

Reflection:

Where have I been handing my emotions to others to manage for me?
How can I respond differently next time I feel triggered?

Mantra:

I take full responsibility for how I feel.
I choose peace, clarity, and conscious response.

Higher Self Trait 4: Self-Compassion

Compassion is strength wrapped in softness.

Self-compassion is the ability to treat yourself with the same kindness, care, and understanding that you would offer someone you deeply love. Your Higher Self knows that you don't need to be perfect to be worthy. It embraces your humanity, your flaws, and your growth with unconditional love.

Your Lower Self, on the other hand, tends to be harsh, critical, and unforgiving. It magnifies your mistakes and whispers:

You're not enough.

You should have done better.

You always mess things up.

These thoughts don't motivate—they create shame, guilt, and paralysis.

But your Higher Self sees mistakes as part of the path.

It says: *You are learning. You are growing. And you are still worthy.*

Self-compassion allows you to release the impossible need for perfection. It gives you space to breathe, to feel, and to begin again without judgment. When you speak to yourself with kindness, you create an inner environment that supports healing, confidence, and progress.

Even when things go wrong, self-compassion helps you stay grounded. It reminds you: *This doesn't define me. This moment doesn't take away my worth.*

It's not weakness—it's strength. It's not avoidance—it's deep alignment. When you stop fighting yourself and start nurturing yourself, everything changes. You stop cycling in shame and start moving forward with grace.

Self-compassion is one of the most powerful traits of the Higher Self—

because it brings you back to your truth:
You are enough, exactly as you are, even as you grow.

Compassion Toward Others

The Higher Self also practices compassion toward *others.* It leads with kindness, chooses understanding over judgment, and responds with love—even when it's hard.

Always be kind.
Be helpful.
And act with love, especially when others are not showing up as their highest selves.

Compassion is the ability to hold space for someone, even when they're lost in their own pain.

It's choosing empathy over ego, softness over criticism, presence over projection.

Operating from your Higher Self means seeing beyond someone's behavior. You recognize their wounds, their conditioning, their unhealed parts—not to excuse poor behavior, but to understand it. To *not carry resentment for it.*

Of course, compassion doesn't mean letting people walk over you. It doesn't mean tolerating mistreatment or ignoring your own needs. **It means knowing that everyone is doing the best they can with the awareness they have.** And instead of reacting with anger or judgment, you respond with grace and emotional maturity.

Compassion comes from a heart that knows how hard life can be—and still chooses love. Your Higher Self sees both others and yourself through the eyes of kindness.

You become someone who uplifts rather than criticizes, who comforts rather than blames.
Sometimes, just sending someone a quiet wave of loving energy can shift everything.

Self-Compassion – Manifestation Reminder
You can't manifest from shame—you manifest from softness.
When you hold space for yourself instead of criticizing yourself, you stay in alignment with love. Self-compassion allows you to keep going, even when you fall. It reminds the universe that you're willing, open, and worthy—no matter where you are in your journey. The softer you are with yourself, the stronger your energy becomes.

Reflection:
Where in my life am I being hard on myself right now?
What would it feel like to offer myself and others understanding instead of judgment?

Mantra:
I give myself permission to be human.
I meet my pain with love and my growth with patience.

Higher Self Trait 5: Self-Discipline

Your Higher Self doesn't wait for motivation—it shows up with commitment. Where the Lower Self finds excuses, your Higher Self makes decisions and follows through.

Self-discipline isn't punishment—it's an act of self-respect. It means honoring the future you desire, even when the present moment tempts you to stay comfortable.

You may already be disciplined in certain areas of life—maybe you're consistent with your work, or you go to the gym regularly. But the Higher Self calls you to bring that level of discipline into every area that matters to your growth. Whether it's your health, your thoughts, your work, your boundaries, or your habits—discipline will always be rewarded.

Sometimes, discipline looks like eating nourishing food. Sometimes, it's choosing to move your body. Other times, it's simply refusing to indulge in negative self-talk.
It's saying: *Even though I feel low right now, I won't give up on myself.*
It's choosing to break patterns that keep you stuck.
It's pulling yourself out of your Lower Self again and again until that no longer feels like home.

It's the part of you that says:
I'm not going to let my temporary emotions sabotage my long-term vision.
It's the energy that gets you up in the morning,
Keeps you aligned when distractions appear, and helps you show up for your dreams—even when it's uncomfortable.

Your Lower Self will whisper things like:

You can do it tomorrow.

Just rest a little more.
It's okay to skip this once.

But your Higher Self responds with clarity:
I know what I want—and I show up for it.

Discipline doesn't mean you never rest—**it means you honor your commitments**. It's what helps you stay focused when distractions appear. It's what keeps you aligned when your emotions fluctuate. It's the practice of keeping your promises to yourself.

No matter what area of life you're working on—career, health, healing, relationships, or mindset—discipline is the bridge between your current self and your highest potential.

Success doesn't come from doing things once—it comes from doing them consistently, especially when it's hard.
And the beautiful thing is: **once you become disciplined, everything starts flowing.** You don't need to chase results—they begin to meet you where you are.

Self-discipline is one of the highest forms of power you can step into. It says:

I choose who I become—every single day

Self-Discipline – Manifestation Reminder

Discipline is a bridge between desire and reality.

Your manifestations need your action. The more consistent you are with your habits, the more you step into the version of you who already has it. Discipline is not pressure—it's self-respect.

Reflection:

Where am I waiting for motivation instead of choosing commitment?

What would shift in my life if I showed up for myself—even when it's uncomfortable?

Mantra:

I don't wait to feel ready—I choose to stay committed.

Discipline is how I honor my dreams in action.

.

Higher Self Trait 6: Taking Aligned Action

Aligned action comes from love, not fear.

Your Higher Self doesn't just act for the sake of being busy—it moves with purpose, direction, and *clarity*.
This is what it means to take aligned or inspired action. It's not about saying yes to everything or hustling just to prove your worth. It's about choosing intentionally. Acting from truth, not urgency. From vision, not pressure.

Aligned action means working **smart**, not just hard.
It's taking on opportunities, projects, and relationships that align with your values and future—not just your current fears or insecurities. It's saying yes to what serves your growth and no to what drains your energy, even if that no is uncomfortable.

Many people confuse action with progress.
They take jobs that pay but leave them empty.
They say yes to events, collaborations, or even relationships that feel wrong in their gut—just to avoid discomfort, judgment, or fear of missing out.

Think of someone who gets married—not because they feel deeply connected, but because they're turning 30 and feel like time is running out. They settle, not out of alignment, but out of fear. It might look like they have it all figured out, but deep down, they're living someone else's timeline. That decision wasn't inspired—it was pressured.

The same happens in careers.
You might take on jobs that don't excite or align with you, just because you're afraid of not having options. Yes, in the beginning, we all say yes to things to gain experience—even work for free at times—but at some

point, you must stop settling and start choosing from worth. If you keep undervaluing your time, people will too.

Aligned action means checking in with yourself before saying yes.
It means asking:

- Is this in alignment with my vision or just feeding my fear?
- Am I choosing this out of clarity—or out of panic, pressure, or comparison?

Your Higher Self trusts that there's always something better when you act from truth.
It knows that saying no to what's misaligned creates space for what's *meant* for you.
It understands that inspired action isn't always fast—but it's always right.

When you take aligned action, you're building a life that reflects your inner world—not one built on other people's timelines or society's expectations. And that's where peace, purpose, and fulfillment live.

Taking Aligned Action – Manifestation Reminder

You don't manifest by doing more—you manifest by doing what aligns. Every action carries energy. When you move from fear, you attract confusion. When you move from truth, you attract miracles. Aligned action is about choosing what matches your future—not your fear. Say no to what drains you, and yes to what expands you.

Reflection

Where in my life am I taking action from fear, pressure, or urgency?

What decisions have I made that didn't feel aligned—but I said yes anyway?

What would my choices look like if I trusted my worth and believed that alignment would bring me everything I need?

Mantra

I choose aligned action. I trust that what is meant for me will meet me when I move with clarity, not fear. I no longer rush—I align.

Higher Self Habit 7: Practicing Inner Peace

Once you begin to love yourself, the next step is learning how to be with yourself—without distraction, without noise, without needing to constantly be somewhere else or achieve something new. This is where mindfulness and inner peace become essential habits in your Higher Self journey.

We often think happiness will come after we fix everything around us. After the job promotion. After the relationship. After we earn enough money or find the perfect home. But peace isn't waiting at the finish line of your goals—it's something you can cultivate right now, in the middle of your current reality.

Mindfulness is the practice of being fully present in the moment. It means noticing your breath, feeling your body, and becoming aware of your thoughts without getting caught up in them. It's reminding yourself that in this exact moment, you are safe, you are whole, and you are not behind.

So many people chase peace, thinking it will come after life becomes easier. But the truth is—life will always have challenges. Peace isn't about perfect conditions. It's about how you show up, no matter what's going on around you.

That's why mindfulness is so powerful. It helps you stop reacting to life impulsively. It calms the mental noise. It teaches you how to hold space for your emotions without being controlled by them. And it brings you back to yourself, over and over again.

You don't need hours of meditation to practice this. Even five minutes a day of sitting quietly, breathing deeply, or simply noticing your surroundings without judgment can make a huge difference in your energy. Over time, you'll start to respond to life with more patience, clarity, and calm.

When you're living in alignment with your Higher Self, peace becomes a priority. You stop waiting for everything to be perfect, and instead, you create moments of stillness and safety within yourself. This is how you begin to feel at home—wherever you are.

Mindfulness helps you:

- Become more emotionally aware and less reactive.
- Feel grounded during stressful situations.
- Break free from the constant need for stimulation.
- Enjoy your own company and find peace within yourself.
- Let go of trying to control everything and simply trust what is.

Peace is not something the world gives you.
It's something you give to yourself—through your presence, your breath, and your daily commitment to being here, now.

Practicing Inner Peace – Manifestation Reminder

Manifestation happens in stillness, not in stress.
When you're calm inside, you become a clear channel for divine guidance. Inner peace doesn't mean avoiding chaos—it means not letting it enter your energy. The quieter your inner world, the faster your outer world aligns.

Reflection:

Where am I rushing, overthinking, or mentally escaping the present moment?
What would it feel like to slow down and be fully here, right now?

Mantra:

I anchor myself in the present moment.
Peace is not something I chase—it's something I choose.

Higher Self Trait 8: Prayer

Prayer is one of the most powerful ways to connect with your Higher Self and the Creator. But it's the *intention* behind your prayer that transforms it.

Most people pray from a place of fear or desperation.
They say things like:
Please make this stop.
Please take this pain away.
Please fix this.

But that kind of prayer isn't rooted in transformation.
It's rooted in control.
It's fear-based.
It's the voice of the Lower Self trying to escape a process that was meant to shape you.

True prayer isn't about removing the pain—it's about receiving the strength to walk through it.

Every challenge, heartbreak, or breakdown you go through is designed to evolve you into a stronger, more aware version of yourself. It may not always make sense in the moment. It might even feel unfair or unbearable. But your soul knows why it's happening—even when your mind doesn't.

According to Kabbalah, your soul chooses every single situation you go through, because it understands exactly what you need to grow, elevate, and transform.

So when you're in a difficult moment, try shifting your prayer.

Instead of saying, *Make it stop*, begin to ask:

- Who do you want me to become through this?
- What do you want me to learn from this?
- What quality is life trying to build in me?
- Creator, give me the certainty to move through this with trust.
- Give me the strength to keep going.
- Help me surrender so I can receive the message behind this pain.

If you're facing health issues, pray for inner healing and clarity.
If you're stuck in confusion, pray for direction and the next right step.
If you're feeling anxious or heartbroken, pray for peace to return.
If you're in a financial breakdown or feel like you're losing control, pray for strength and guidance—and trust that the breakdown is often the beginning of your breakthrough.

Prayer isn't about pleading or begging the Universe to save you—
It's about **aligning your energy with it.**

And the Universe always listens.
But in order to hear it, you must become still.
In order to receive its whispers, you must be willing to surrender.

Make it a practice to speak to the Creator every day.
It doesn't have to be long or perfect.
Even just five minutes—spoken out loud or in your mind, through messy words or silent tears—is enough.
What matters most is your connection.

You can say something simple, like:
Creator, I know this situation was given to me because, somewhere deep inside, I can handle it. I may not understand it yet, but I trust I will in time. Please give

me the certainty to keep going. Please give me peace. Please give me the strength to hold on—until I see the light.

This is how true transformation begins.
You don't need to fix everything at once.

You don't need the pain to disappear overnight.
You just need to stay connected—to something deeper than fear.

Your Higher Self doesn't panic.
It doesn't rush to control or fix.
It knows how to breathe.
It knows how to listen.
And it knows how to trust.

Prayer is your reminder that you are never walking alone.

Prayer – Manifestation Reminder

Prayer is not just asking—it's aligning.

When you pray with certainty instead of desperation, you shift into faith. Prayer isn't begging for change—it's declaring your trust. The moment you stop asking "Why me?" and start asking "Guide me," the universe moves with you.

Reflection:

Am I using prayer to escape my pain—or to ask for the strength to transform it?

What would shift if I prayed not out of fear, but from trust?

Mantra:

My prayers are not cries for rescue—they are invitations for divine alignment.

I ask not just for outcomes, but for guidance, strength, and transformation.

Higher Self Trait 9: Surrender to the Universe

Surrender is not giving up—it's handing it over to a greater power with trust.

Sometimes, despite all your effort, planning, and overthinking—nothing moves.

And in those moments, your Higher Self gently whispers:

Let go. You don't have to carry this alone.

Surrender is a beautiful, sacred practice. It's when you finally release control —not because you've failed, but because you recognize that there's a greater intelligence at work. It's when you've done your part and now allow life, the Creator, the Universe—whatever you believe in—to step in and guide the way.

Surrender says: *I've done what I can. I trust what comes next.*

This isn't weakness.

It's the deepest form of strength.

Because it means you trust—truly trust—that you are not alone in this world. That you are held, supported, protected. That your path is unfolding for you, even when you cannot see what's ahead.

Instead of constantly trying to fix, control, or force outcomes, you soften. You breathe. You say:

This is what it is. I've given my best. Now, I surrender. Show me the way.

And something magical begins to happen.

You stop resisting life.

You stop swimming against the current.

You allow space for peace, for miracles, for guidance to reach you.

Surrender doesn't mean you stop taking action.
It means you take action from trust, not desperation.
You let go of the outcome, knowing that the right result will meet you when the time is right.

Your Higher Self knows when to surrender.
It doesn't fight the timing. It doesn't chase what isn't meant.
It simply says: *I trust the unfolding of my life.*
And that trust changes everything.

Surrender – Manifestation Reminder

Surrender isn't giving up—it's getting in flow.
When you let go of how and when your desire should show up, you make space for divine timing. Surrender says, *Ive done my part. Now I trust the universe to do the rest.* That's when the magic rushes in.

Reflection

Where in my life am I still trying to control what is out of my hands?
What would happen if I trusted that things are working out even when I can't see the result yet?
Can I soften into the unknown and allow myself to be guided?

Mantra

I surrender what I cannot control. I am guided, supported, and held by a force greater than me. I trust the timing of my life.

Higher Self Trait 10: Detachment

Detachment doesn't mean you stop caring.
It doesn't mean you walk through life cold or emotionless.

It means you stop clinging. You stop trying to control what was never yours to control.

To understand detachment, you first have to understand attachment.

Attachment is when you tie your happiness, peace, or self-worth to a specific outcome, person, or situation. It's when your sense of wholeness depends on how things unfold or how someone treats you.
It sounds like:

If this relationship doesn't work, I won't be okay.
If I don't manifest this goal soon, I've failed.
I need their love, attention, or approval to feel enough.

Attachment blurs your vision.
It makes you ignore red flags.
It convinces you to hold on to people who aren't aligned, or to force things that aren't flowing—because you're more afraid of letting go than trusting what's meant for you.

When you're attached, you don't see clearly. You don't hear your intuition. You don't create space for what's truly right for you—because you're fixated on what you think must happen.

That's where detachment becomes the gateway to peace.

Your Higher Self is deeply loving.
It desires connection, success, expansion, and fulfillment.

But it doesn't base its happiness on any of it.
It knows: I *can want something deeply... and still let it go if it's not aligned.*

That's the power of detachment.
It's knowing that your peace is rooted inside you—not in outcomes, not in people, not in approval or timelines.

When you operate from detachment:

- You release the need to control how things unfold.
- You trust that what's meant for you will come—and what's not will fall away, even if it hurts in the moment.
- You no longer make your desire your identity.

Instead of *I need this to be happy*, you shift into:
I would love for this to happen—but my happiness is not dependent on it.

And here's something you've probably felt before—when you meet someone who is truly detached, their energy is light.
They're not seeking something from you. They're not trying to control or impress. They show up whole, calm, and connected.
Their energy feels magnetic, clear, and effortless.
Those people? They're usually deeply surrendered. They trust life. They let things flow.
And because they're not chasing or grasping, you feel safe around them.

Now contrast that with someone who's clingy, needy, or obsessed with outcomes—their energy feels heavy, anxious, and draining.
You can sense it. Because energy doesn't lie.

Detachment is lightness. Detachment is trust. Detachment is peace.

And ironically, the more detached you are, the more quickly what's right for you flows into your life.
Because you're no longer operating from fear, control, or lack—you're operating from grounded, radiant trust.

Letting go doesn't mean giving up.
It means trusting deeper.
It means honoring your own energy so deeply that you'd rather wait for alignment than force what isn't real.

That is the freedom your Higher Self lives from.
And it's available to you the moment you stop attaching your peace to anything outside of you.

Detachment – Manifestation Reminder

Detachment is the final step of true manifestation.

When you detach, you're not giving up—you're giving space. You show the universe you trust the outcome. Neediness repels. Faith attracts. Let go of how and when, and let your energy say, *I know it's already mine.*

Reflection:

Where am I holding on so tightly that I'm creating tension instead of trust?

What would shift if I believed I could love, want, and desire deeply—while still letting go?

Mantra:

I am allowed to want without needing.

I release what I cannot control and make space for what's aligned.

Higher Self Trait 11: Staying Calm in Chaos

One of the greatest powers you can develop in life is the ability to stay calm in chaos.
To remain steady when life doesn't go as planned.
To choose peace—even when everything around you feels unstable.

Your Higher Self holds this quality deeply.
It doesn't get shaken by circumstances.
It doesn't spiral when uncertainty hits.
It remains grounded in trust—even when the path forward isn't clear.

Because inner peace isn't about having a life without chaos.
It's about staying calm in the middle of the storm.

Your Higher Self carries peace not because everything is perfect, but because it trusts that everything is unfolding exactly as it's meant to. It understands that panic doesn't lead to clarity—presence does.

When you're anchored in your inner world, the external world loses its power to shake you.
You don't react impulsively to bad news.
You don't spiral when something doesn't go your way.
You breathe. You pause. You reflect. You respond.

This ability to stay calm in the storm is one of life's most powerful spiritual secrets.

Because challenges will always come.
Uncertainty will always show up.
But your nervous system doesn't have to live in survival mode.

When you remain calm:

- You can think clearly.
- You receive guidance from your intuition.
- You access solutions you wouldn't have seen in panic.
- You respond with wisdom instead of reactivity.
- You stay kind—to yourself and to others—even in the middle of conflict.

Reacting from overwhelm creates disconnection.
Your nervous system goes into overdrive.
You imagine worst-case scenarios.
You speak from fear.
And that negative energy blocks your flow. It blocks your clarity.
It makes everything feel heavier than it really is.

You become someone else—a version of you driven by emotion, stress, or survival.

But when you stay calm, your energy stays clean.
You don't overreact, overexplain, or overanalyze.
You move from your center.
You hold yourself with grace.

And people feel that.
They feel safe in your presence because you feel safe within yourself.

Inner peace is not weakness. It's strength.
It's the ability to say: *Even if this is hard, I will go through it in peace.*

It's learning to soothe your inner world—no matter what's happening outside of you.
And yes, it takes practice. Especially if you've been taught to react, to worry, to fix

But every time you choose calm over chaos, you become stronger. Every time you choose peace, you invite wisdom, healing, and solutions.

And your overall life begins to change.

You no longer live in a rush.
You stop comparing.
You feel lighter, more aligned, more available to life.
You hear your intuition. You enjoy the moment.
Your energy is magnetic.
The quality of your life rises.

So the next time you feel overwhelmed, ask yourself:
How would my Higher Self handle this right now?

That one question can bring you back to center.
Because the truth is: *Being unbothered is power.*
Staying calm in chaos opens the door to flow, clarity, and miracles.

You're not here to be consumed by stress.
You're here to lead your energy.
And that begins with choosing peace.

My Own Journey with This

I used to be a calm person in many situations—but when it came to deeper emotional challenges, I would sometimes react without thinking. And honestly, it made me feel even worse than before.

But over time, I learned how to stay calm even when everything around me was falling apart.
I reminded myself: *Even if this storm comes, I will remain still. I will trust.*
It didn't happen overnight. But with time, I practiced.

Now, even if I do react emotionally—it only lasts a few minutes.
Sometimes five, maybe ten.
And often, not at all. Because I remember who I am. I remember my Higher Self.

This shift has helped me move through heartbreaks, failures, big life changes, and more—without losing myself.
It changed everything.

Staying Calm in Chaos – Manifestation Reminder

Your energy in the storm determines what comes next.
When you stay grounded during uncertainty, you stay aligned with your vision. Reacting from panic creates delay. Responding with calm creates clarity. The more peaceful you are in chaos, the faster you receive what's meant for you.

Reflection:

What situations tend to shake my inner peace the most—and why?
How can I lead myself with calm instead of reacting from chaos?

Mantra:

Even in the storm, I choose peace.
My calm is my power, and I lead my life from within.

Higher Self Trait 12: Listen to Your Intuition

Your intuition is the quiet, inner knowing that guides you beyond logic. It's that gut feeling—that whisper in your soul that says, *This feels right* or *Something's off.* Your Higher Self is deeply connected to this voice. It doesn't rush. It listens, feels, and trusts what it senses—even when it doesn't make immediate sense.

We often override our intuition with fear, logic, or the noise of other people's opinions.

How many times have you said, *I knew I shouldn't have done that*, after ignoring your gut feeling?

That was your Higher Self trying to speak to you.

Meditation is one of the most powerful ways to reconnect with it. When you meditate, you become present. You learn to quiet your overactive mind and enter stillness. And in that stillness, your intuition has space to come through.

We are constantly receiving messages, emotions, signs, and ideas through our intuition—but when we're too caught up in the outside world, always thinking, always listening to too many voices, we miss them.

Oprah Winfrey calls it *the whisper*—that subtle, inner nudge.

And it truly is a whisper from the Creator, guiding you gently toward what's aligned with your truth.

Always stay open to receiving messages and guidance from your intuition.

Some of the best ideas I've ever had came to me this way—effortlessly.

Solutions I would have never thought of, ideas I couldn't have strategized or planned—just came to me.

And I knew in that moment: this wasn't from my mind, it was from something higher.

It was from the univierse.
Intuition doesn't always show up with logic. Sometimes it leads you in a direction no one else understands.

You might get a strong feeling to leave a relationship.
To say no to a big opportunity.
To take a leap when others say you're crazy.
But if your intuition says it's right—you must learn to trust that.

Even if it doesn't make sense to the outside world, your soul always knows.

That's why having a strong, healthy relationship with yourself is so important—because trusting your intuition *is* trusting yourself.

In fact, the idea to write this book came from my intuition. I was reading a book, and suddenly the message just came. I had never planned to write a book. I'm not a trained writer. I never studied it. And I wrote it in English, even though it's not my first language. At the time, I was living in India and nothing about the idea made logical sense.

But I didn't ignore the whisper.
I sat with it.
I listened.
And I followed.

And now—you're holding this book in your hands.

That's the power of intuition.
It gives you the best ideas. The best solutions. The boldest moves.
It's the quiet voice that knows what you need before your mind can explain why.

Always trust it.

Listening to Intuition – Manifestation Reminder

Your intuition is the voice of alignment.

Every time you ignore it, you delay your destiny. Every time you follow it, you collapse timelines. Manifestation isn't logic—it's energy. And your intuition always knows what your mind hasn't figured out yet.

Reflection:

When was the last time I listened to my intuition—and what happened?

Where in my life am I being guided right now, even if it doesn't make logical sense?

Mantra:

I trust the whispers within.

My intuition is divine guidance, and I choose to follow it with courage.

Higher Self Trait 13: Trusting Yourself (Self-Trust)

Self-trust is closely linked to your intuition—but it's also much more than that.

It's the relationship you have with yourself when things are uncertain, when life doesn't go to plan, when you're in pain, or when the future feels completely unclear.
It's the voice inside you that says, *Even though I don't know what's next, I know I'll be okay.*

Self-trust isn't something you're born with.
It's something you build—**moment by moment, decision by decision, conversation by conversation—with yourself.**

You build it:

- When you're going through heartbreak and still tell yourself, This pain won't break me. I will find love again.
- When you're facing uncertainty and whisper, Even though I don't have the answers, I trust that they're coming.
- When you feel lost in your career or purpose and say, Even here, in the unknown, I choose to believe in myself.
- When your manifestations are delayed, and you remind yourself, What's meant for me is on its way.

Self-trust means learning to be the **voice of strength and reassurance in your own life**—even when no one else is giving it to you.
It's choosing to believe in your decisions, your timing, and your path—even when it doesn't make sense to anyone else.

It's telling yourself:

I may not know what's next, but I trust myself to figure it out.
I trust that the choices I make now are leading me exactly where I need to be.
I trust that if something didn't work out, it's because something better is coming.

Self-trust isn't about knowing what's going to happen.
It's about knowing that you will walk yourself through whatever happens —with courage, with grace, and with love. And yes—it's deeply connected to self-love.

Because the more you love yourself, the more you believe in yourself.
It's also connected to intuition.
Because the more you trust yourself, the more clearly you can hear your inner guidance.

And it's also built through self-talk—the words you say to yourself when no one else is around.
So when you're going through a storm—whether it's heartbreak, loss, rejection, failure, or confusion—remind yourself:

This moment does not define me. I trust myself to rise again.

The moment you trust yourself, the moment you make yourself safe to lean on, everything else starts to align.

You walk into rooms with confidence. You speak your truth with courage. You take action without constantly needing reassurance. **Self-trust is the foundation that connects every other trait of your Higher Self.** And once you strengthen it, you become unstoppable.

Self-Trust – Manifestation Reminder

The universe can't give you more if you don't trust yourself to receive it. Self-trust is the root of worthiness. The more you believe in your ability to handle, hold, and honor what you manifest, the faster it arrives. Doubt delays. Trust delivers.

Reflection:

In what area of my life am I still doubting myself—and what would shift if I chose to trust myself fully, even in the unknown?

Mantra:

Even when I don't know what's next, I trust myself to walk through it.
I am my own anchor, and I choose to believe in me.

Higher Self Trait 14: Manifestation Mindset

A manifestation mindset is about expecting the best. It's choosing better thoughts in each moment, even when you're unsure. It's choosing to move through the unknown with faith and certainty that what you want will come to you—even if it doesn't look like it yet.

It also means being open to receiving. Because if you're not open, how can the doors open for you?

Blessings don't always come from the direction you expect. They often come through people—or even strangers—you never saw coming. That's why it's important to stay open, stay receptive, and stay connected to your heart. Your heart always knows what's right.

When you want to manifest miracles, you have to tune into your Higher Self and trust that what you're going through is shaping you. Many people try to manifest without becoming the person they need to be. That's what causes delays—or blocks the blessing entirely.

You can't become a CEO without developing the mindset and energy of one. You can't think in lack and expect to receive abundance. You can't be the light for others if you're not being that light for yourself. And you definitely can't attract a beautiful relationship if the one you have with yourself is full of doubt, fear, or chaos.

That's why I wrote this book—to help you bring awareness to who you are being, and to help you align with the version of you who's ready to receive.

To manifest, you have to commit—to your thoughts, your habits, and your daily actions. Manifesting is easy when you align with the version of you who already has it. You don't manifest through force or stress—you manifest through becoming.

And yes, that sometimes means going through challenges. The universe might send situations that stretch you, so you can grow into someone who can hold the blessing you asked for. You might not want to hear it, but it's true—your growth is part of your manifestation.

Imagine going through a really hard time and still choosing to think positively. Still choosing to believe. That's when you become unstoppable. That's when you become powerful. And that's when your manifestations arrive faster—because you earned them with your faith.

Like I said in the trait on peace: being calm in the storm makes you powerful. Because deep down, you know everything will work out.

Doubts kill dreams. You have to eliminate them. Yes, we all have doubts—but when you identify them and release them, you create space for what you've asked for.

Speak to the universe directly and say:

I can't see anything happening right now, but I trust you.
I know you'll make my dreams come true.
I know you're supporting me.

That's called faith. And faith is always rewarded.

Manifestation always works. But the truth is—you can also manifest what you don't want if your energy is focused on lack, fear, or insecurity. If you carry self-worth wounds and believe you're unlucky or that good things can't happen to you, that's exactly what you'll attract. Your energy says no to the blessings before they even reach you.

You have to train yourself to think the thoughts you want to believe. Even when the negative ones come, catch them. Say to yourself:

My Higher Self doesn't think like that. I choose to believe.

In this world, we're often taught that only a few people get to be lucky—those with wealth, connections, or powerful fathers.

But let me tell you something:

You also have a Godfather.
And your Godfather is the Universe.
You may not have had the same upbringing.
You may not have had it easy.
But that does not make you a victim.
You are deeply supported.

And that's something you practice every day.
If you're not used to feeling abundant, remind yourself daily:

I am worthy. I am valuable. I deserve everything I desire.

You may not have a physical Godfather.
But you have one in energy.
And once you connect to that energy and begin becoming the version of you who is ready to receive—your life will begin to shift.

I promise you—once you start throwing your doubts away, once you love yourself unconditionally, once you start choosing your Higher Self again and again—your relationships will change.

Your finances will improve.
Your health will get better.
Your whole life will elevate.

When you trust the Universe, when you trust the Creator, and when you let go energetically—that's when the Universe starts working for you.

So whenever you want to manifest something—have certainty.
Have big dreams.
Have many dreams.
Because everything you want is available to you.

Think of all the people who created the most beautiful things in this world.
It started with one simple thing:
A thought.

That thought became an idea.
That idea became a plan.

My Manifestation Journey

I want to share something personal with you about my journey with manifestation. One thing that truly shifted things for me—what brought in the most powerful manifestations—was not just the belief. It was the change I made. It was who I became in the process.

My biggest manifestations came when I made bold, sometimes painful decisions.

I had to let go of friendships that were toxic and draining. At the time, I didn't even realize how unhealthy they were—because I hadn't yet learned my worth.

But when I finally walked away and reconnected with myself through self-love, self-trust, and inner work, everything started shifting.

I began attracting aligned relationships, deeply fulfilling friendships, and work that resonated with who I truly was.

And that's what manifestation is all about.

Not just asking for what you want—**but becoming the version of yourself who can receive it.**

It's in the daily practice.

It's in saying no when something doesn't feel right.

It's in staying true to yourself, even when it's hard.

It's in learning to walk away from anything that disconnects you from your peace.

When I moved from Germany to India to pursue acting, I left behind everything—my home, my friends, my comfort zone.

I knew no one. I had no guarantees.

It's only been a few years, but it has been one of the most challenging and transformative journeys of my life.

I faced setbacks. I met toxic people. I felt deeply alone at times.

But I trusted myself.
I trusted my intuition.
I listened to that small inner voice, even when it didn't make sense.
And step by step—through workshops, connections, aligned opportunities—I found my way.

Not only did I begin working in the industry I came for, I also started doing what I always dreamed of: **hosting my Manifest It events**, where I could help people reconnect with themselves and their own power.
And then, of course, this book—like I mentioned before, I'm not a writer. I never studied it. I was never particularly good at it. And English is a language I only started learning when I moved to India.
But when the idea came, I knew I had to do it.
And what I realized is this:

Manifesting is not forcing—it's aligning.

I was disciplined. I was consistent. And I was honest about who I wanted to be. When I stopped settling for people or projects that didn't align with my values, everything started to flow.

Yes, I lost people.
Yes, I had to sit in the discomfort of being alone.
But I trusted that what was meant for me would come. And it did.

That's what I want you to understand.

Manifestation is becoming.
Becoming the version of you who already has the love, the peace, the abundance, the fulfillment.

It's about taking aligned action, choosing self-worth, practicing self-love, and having unwavering trust in yourself—even when things don't make sense yet.

I've known about manifestation since I was a teenager. But for a long time, I forced it. I wasn't patient. I worked hard—but not always smart. I was insecure, filled with self-doubt, and constantly seeking validation.

And that's why I wrote this book. Because I've lived it. I've been through the struggle. And I want you to know:

There is so much abundance in this world.
So many beautiful relationships.
So many magical opportunities.
So much love. So much money. So many lucky moments.
And all of it is available to you—**when you start believing that it is.**

Manifest from a place of alignment, not fear.
Become the version of you who already has it.
And choose to connect with your Higher Self—again and again, every single day.

Speaking It Into Existence - Manifestation Mindset

Speaking your desires out loud is not wishful thinking—it's spiritual alignment. It's a clear signal to the Universe that you're not waiting for life to "happen" to you.

You're consciously co-creating it with your words, your energy, and your presence.

Every word you speak carries power.

Your Higher Self understands this truth—and speaks life into dreams before there's any physical proof.

Whether it's the dream job, a deep love, meaningful success, magnetic confidence, beautiful conversations, unexpected blessings, or the home you've always wanted—

It all begins with what you say.
What you say to yourself.
What you say to the Universe.

You must speak it into existence until it becomes the most natural truth in your world—even if your current reality doesn't reflect it yet.

You don't have to wait until it shows up to believe it.
You speak it first—and then you rise into it.

Examples of Speaking from Your Higher Self

- I am magnetic to aligned opportunities and people.
- I am doing work that lights up my soul and brings me abundance.
- I trust that the love I desire is already making its way to me.
- I am confident, clear, and calm in every conversation I have.
- Everything I desire is meant for me and is already unfolding perfectly.

- Money flows to me in ways I never expected, and I receive it with ease.
-

Abundance Mindset - Speaking It Into Existence
When you're in abundance, you relax.
You let go.
You trust that if one door closes—infinite more are opening.
Some haven't even been built yet.
But they're already on their way to you.

Examples of how you can shift your perspective and choose better words to speak it into existence:

Love & Relationships
An abundant mindset says:
If someone isn't aligned with me, I release them lovingly.
I know deeper, healthier, more expansive love is available.
Lower Self says:
What if I never find this again?
Higher Self says:
There is love everywhere. The right kind finds me when I'm being myself.

Work & Purpose
An abundant mindset says:
If this job isn't for me, something better is.
Lower Self says:
I have to hold onto this even if it drains me.
Higher Self says:
I am meant to do work that lights me up and supports me. And it exists.

Money & Resources
Lower Self says:
What if there's not enough?
Higher Self says:
Money is energy—and I'm open to receiving it in ways I never imagined.

Time & Opportunities
Lower Self says:
It's too late for me.
Higher Self says:
I'm right on time for everything meant for me. Life is always unfolding in my favor.

When you live with an abundance mindset, you stop looking at life as a competition.
You start seeing it as a canvas.

There's space for all of us.
There's success, love, freedom, and joy available to you right now.
You don't need to steal it, chase it, or fight for it.
You just have to *align with it.*

Manifestation Mindset – Manifestation Reminder

Manifestation isn't a trick—it's a frequency.

When your mindset is rooted in faith, possibility, and belief, the universe responds. You don't attract what you want—you attract what you believe. Think like it's already yours, and your energy will begin pulling it in.

Your Task:

Write down what you want to speak into existence.

Don't hold back.

Be honest. Be bold. Be excited.

Once you know what you want, turn it into affirmations or mantras that align with your future self—and start speaking them aloud.

Speak them with love.

Speak them with certainty.

Speak them like they've already arrived.

Because when you speak from alignment, the universe listens.

Higher Self Trait 15: Perception Creates Reality

You can't always choose your situation—but you can choose how you see it. And that changes everything.

Your perception is not just how you see the world—it's how you experience it.
The lens you choose in any situation will determine the emotional and energetic reality you live in.

You can be in the middle of a challenge and still choose to see a little light —and even that small shift changes everything. Because the moment you stop seeing your struggle as punishment and start seeing it as a moment to navigate, your power returns.

Imagine two people going through the exact same problem:
One chooses a **lack perspective**—they feel defeated, heavy, and overwhelmed. The other chooses an **abundance perspective**—not because things are perfect, but because they choose to believe there's a way *through.*

They both face the same situation—but the one with the abundance mindset is calmer, more open, and more connected to possibility.
They say: *This is the situation. Now, how can I work with it?*
They move forward from a place of solution—not panic.

They don't let the challenge define their energy.
They treat it as a tool, like a puzzle or a game, asking:

1. How can I shift this?
2. What can I learn from this?
3. What's this teaching me?

Meanwhile, the person with a lack perspective may first spiral into fear, blame, and emotional chaos. It takes them longer to find clarity—not because the problem is worse, but because their perception makes it *feel* heavier.

This is the power of perspective.
It doesn't erase the struggle—but it transforms your relationship with it.
It shortens your suffering.
It accelerates your healing.
It opens you up to receive the very solution you're looking for.

Choosing to see through the lens of abundance, growth, and trust allows you to move through life with grace—even when things are messy.
Because you're no longer fighting the moment. You're flowing with it.

And that is the energy your Higher Self lives in.

Perception Creates Reality – Manifestation Reminder

What you focus on expands.

Two people can go through the same situation—but the one who sees it with faith, hope, and possibility unlocks the path forward. Your perspective shapes your energy, and your energy shapes what you attract. Choose to see the light—and your reality will start to reflect it.

Reflection

How am I currently perceiving the challenges in my life?

Is my mindset helping me move forward—or keeping me stuck?

What would shift if I chose to see just a little bit of light in this situation?

Mantra

I choose to see with faith. I choose to see with love. My perception creates my reality, and I choose peace—even in the process.

Higher Self Trait 16: Gratitude

Gratitude is the ability to fully appreciate the present moment and everything it holds. It is one of the highest vibrational emotions, and when we embrace it, we align ourselves with abundance and positivity. The Higher Self is rooted in gratitude, always seeking the good in every situation—no matter how challenging it may seem.

Many people tend to focus only on big achievements, overlooking the beauty of everyday things that come easily. We often forget to appreciate the roof over our head, the food we eat, the relationships we have, and even the small comforts of life. These are things we might take for granted—yet they are part of the foundation of our present happiness. When we start recognizing the value of these simple gifts, we feel more grounded, fulfilled, and connected to the present moment.

Gratitude is a powerful force because it reminds us that we already have so much to be thankful for. It shifts us from a mindset of scarcity—where we constantly think about what we don't have—into a mindset of abundance, where we focus on everything we do have. This shift makes us feel whole, complete, and satisfied—not in need of anything outside ourselves to feel better.

In my eyes, gratitude is one of the most powerful practices you can adopt —not just being thankful for the *big* things, but for *everything* in your life. Be grateful for yourself, for what you've overcome, for who you are right now, and for everything that's come your way. This practice of gratitude strengthens your connection to your Higher Self and opens up space for more goodness to flow into your life.

When you truly embody gratitude, you are also aligning with the Law of Attraction. By appreciating what you have in the present moment, you invite more blessings into your life. The universe can only work with us when we are present, open, and receptive. A state of gratitude ensures you are ready to receive more—because you are already abundant in the now.

You don't need to constantly chase what you think you're lacking. Instead, you attract more—**because you already recognize the richness of what you have.**

Be grateful for your future and your manifestations

While it's essential to be deeply grateful for what you already have—your breath, your growth, your journey—there's also magic in being grateful for what's *on its way.*

When you combine gratitude for the present with gratitude for the future, you shift into a state of **aliveness, excitement, and deep trust.** You begin to align with your manifestations before they arrive. You say, *Thank you for the love that's coming into my life*, or *Thank you for the opportunities that are already finding me.'*

This kind of gratitude opens your heart and expands your energy. It tells the universe: *I trust you. I believe it's already happening.* And in that moment, you stop chasing and start attracting.

Gratitude for the future is a practice of faith. It moves you from lack into *overflow*—from doubt into *deservingness.* And it invites your manifestations to come faster, because you're already living in the energy of receiving.

Gratitude is also a conversation with the Universe

Gratitude isn't only about listing what you're thankful for—it's also about **talking to the universe and acknowledging what's working.** When something good happens, even if it's something small—like getting an upgrade, a kind message, or a moment of ease—say it out loud:

Thank you, Universe. This is amazing. I love this—please send me more of it.

This simple practice supercharges your manifestations. It tells the universe:
I see what you gave me, and I'm open to receiving more.
You're no longer passively hoping—*you're actively co-creating.*

Even when something shows up that's close to what you want, but not exactly, you can still speak to the universe with gratitude and clarity. For example:
Thank you for this experience. It's beautiful and I appreciate it—and what I truly desire is something a little more like this...

You're not complaining—*you're refining.* You're showing gratitude while also staying connected to your vision.

This is the perfect blend of **faith and clarity, receiving and asking.**
It's not just gratitude—it's a loving, powerful dialogue with the energy that's guiding you.

Gratitude – Manifestation Reminder

Gratitude is a magnet for miracles.

When you're truly grateful—not just for what you have, but also for what's coming—you move into deep alignment. Gratitude tells the universe, I *trust you*. That trust creates space for even more to arrive.

Reflection:

What in my life right now have I forgotten to be grateful for?

What future desires can I begin thanking the universe for—as if they are already on their way?

When something beautiful or exciting happens, do I pause to acknowledge it and tell the universe, "Yes, more of this please"?

Mantra:

Thank you for what I have. Thank you for what's coming. Thank you for what keeps flowing to me. I am always guided, always supported, and always grateful.

Higher Self Trait 17: Being Authentic

Being authentic is the highest form of self-respect.

Being authentic simply means being true to yourself—to who you really are, what you believe in, and what you feel called to do. It's about being honest with yourself and the world, even if it's uncomfortable. Even if people don't understand. Even if they talk about you.

Especially when you're growing, healing, or changing—people will have opinions. Let them. Let them wonder, judge, or guess. That's not your business. Your only responsibility is to **stay true to the version of you that feels most honest and free.**

You don't need to fit into anyone else's vision for your life.
You don't need to copy trends or follow what's popular online if it doesn't resonate with you.
You don't have to prove yourself to anyone—just *be yourself*, fully and unapologetically.

Do the things your heart is drawn to. Follow your own rhythm. Speak your truth, wear what you love, live how you want. That's authenticity.

And the beautiful thing is—when you live this way, people can feel it.
Authenticity is magnetic.
It's not about perfection. It's about alignment.

Your Lower Self wants to be liked. It wants to blend in, to be accepted. It fears judgment.
But your Higher Self wants to be real. It wants to express, create, and exist without needing permission.

This trait connects deeply to self-love—because being authentic is one of

the greatest acts of love you can give to yourself.
It's a gift. A declaration. A decision to say: *I am enough as I am.*

So stay true.
Be bold.
Do it your way.
And let the world adjust.

Authenticity – Manifestation Reminder
You can't manifest the life you want by being someone you're not. The more you honor your truth, the more aligned your reality becomes. Authenticity is magnetic—because it vibrates with power, clarity, and freedom. Be you, fully—and your desires will recognize you.

Reflection:
Where am I still hiding parts of myself to be accepted or approved?
What would it feel like to show up fully as who I am—without editing, shrinking, or performing?

Mantra:
My truth is my power.
I choose to be fully, freely, and unapologetically me.

Higher Self Trait 18: Embody Your Worth

To embody your worth means to fully accept and express your inherent value in everything you do. It's about aligning with the truth that you deserve love, respect, success, and abundance—*simply because you exist.* Not because you're constantly striving for validation or approval.

When you embody your worth, you stop seeking approval from others.
You no longer feel the need to prove yourself or convince anyone of your value.
You understand that your worth isn't contingent on meeting someone else's expectations or standards.
It's rooted in your core identity—it's simply who you are.

Embodying your worth doesn't mean you're perfect.
It means you've accepted yourself, imperfections and all.
It's about honoring your feelings, setting boundaries, and standing up for what you deserve—without apology.
It's the quiet confidence—the knowing that you can be both imperfect and worthy at the same time.

For so many, self-worth is often tied to external circumstances—money, relationships, accomplishments, or appearance.
But when you embody your worth, you realize none of these things truly define you.
You define them.

When you live from this truth, everything shifts.
You begin to expect respect in your relationships.
You receive kindness with grace.
And you stop settling for anything less than what aligns with your highest vision of yourself.

For example, in relationships, when you embody your worth, you don't stay in situations where you feel undervalued or unappreciated.
You choose people who uplift you, who honor you, and who treat you as the valuable person that you are.
You set boundaries that protect your peace and prioritize your well-being.

In your career, when you embody your worth, you don't accept roles that don't align with your talents and desires.
You know you deserve opportunities that challenge you, recognize your gifts, and allow you to grow.
You don't wait for permission to succeed—you claim it confidently.

Most importantly, when you embody your worth, you stop shrinking to fit.
You stop dimming your light to make others feel comfortable.
You stop apologizing for your success, your power, or your greatness.
You show up as the most authentic, confident version of yourself—
and in doing so, you give others permission to do the same.

This is the essence of embodying your worth:
Walking through life unapologetically, knowing you deserve all the good that comes your way.
It's a practice.
A daily reminder to honor your value.

When you align with this trait, you create a ripple effect that not only transforms your own life—but inspires others to rise.
Your worth is already within you.
Your only job is to embody it fully—and let the world witness the magnificent person you truly are.

Gaining Confidence Through Embodying Your Worth

When you start truly embodying your worth, everything about you shifts.
You walk differently. You talk differently.
There's a quiet power in you—a glow, a groundedness, an unshakable presence.

You don't need to prove anything.
You don't need to announce it.
Your energy says it all.

That smile, that posture, that peaceful confidence—it comes from doing the inner work.
It comes from self-respect, self-love, and alignment with who you really are.

And let's be clear: knowing your worth is not arrogance.
It's not about thinking you're better than others.
It's about knowing *you don't need to shrink or beg to be valued.*

People who deeply know their worth move with clarity.
They know what they deserve.
They make decisions based on alignment, not fear.
And that energy?

It's magnetic. It's beautiful. It's deeply attractive.
Because when you embody your worth, you show others what's possible.
You become an example of someone who isn't chasing love, attention, or approval—you're radiating it from within.

Embodying Your Worth – Manifestation Reminder

Your worth sets the tone for what you allow in.

You don't receive what you wish for—you receive what you believe you deserve. When you embody your worth, you speak differently, choose differently, and attract differently. The world meets you at your standard.

Reflection:

Where in my life am I still accepting less than I deserve?

What would shift if I fully owned my worth and stopped settling?

Mantra:

I know my worth, and I no longer shrink to be accepted.

I am the table—I bring the energy, the value, and the vision.

Higher Self Trait 19: Vision

Your Higher Self has vision.

It sees beyond your current circumstances and limitations. It doesn't define you by what's happening now—but by what's possible.

Vision gives you direction.

It helps you remember where you're going, even when the path feels unclear or hard.

Most people without vision get stuck. They get pulled into survival, distractions, or doubt.

But your Higher Self knows how to zoom out—to see the bigger picture.

It knows your pain has purpose.

It knows your setbacks are setup points for something greater.

It helps you hold on, even when things don't make sense yet.

And vision doesn't always come with perfect clarity.

Sometimes it's just a feeling—a deep knowing that you're meant for more.

And that knowing is enough to take the next step.

You don't need to see the whole staircase—just trust the direction.

Everything is possible.

We often think in limited ways based on what we've seen or been told.

But to connect with your Higher Self, you have to stretch your imagination.

You have to believe in something greater.

Vision asks you to create from faith, not fear.

To build something new, you must look beyond what already exists.

If you're creating a life no one around you has lived—it won't look familiar.

And that's okay.

Think about it—there was once a time with no mobile phones, no high-speed internet, no social media.
Someone envisioned all of that—and created it.

Before that, when the Wright brothers—Orville and Wilbur—dared to believe humans could fly, people laughed.
They said it was ridiculous.
But the Wright brothers held onto their vision and brought airplanes into existence.

Today, flying across continents in hours is normal.
That's the power of vision.

So have a big vision.
Don't limit yourself.
This world is full of abundance, ideas, and creation—waiting for you to claim it.

You don't have to base your vision on what's been done before.
You're here to create what's never been seen.

Because vision isn't just about dreaming

—

It's about living like your future already belongs to you.

Vision – Manifestation Reminder

Your vision is a preview of what's already possible.

Hold it. Honor it. Believe in it—especially when no one else sees it. Your vision is your energetic blueprint. The more clearly you see it, the more clearly the universe can deliver it.

Reflection:

Do I have a clear vision for the life I truly desire—or am I living by default?

What would my future look like if I gave myself full permission to dream boldly?

Mantra:

I hold the vision, even when I can't yet see the results.

My future is already written—I'm just aligning with it.

Chapter 4:
Connecting and Manifesting from Your Higher Self

You don't attract what you want. You attract what you are.

– Dr. Wayne Dyer

Now that you understand your Higher and Lower Self, it's time to put this awareness into practice. This book isn't something you read once and forget—it's something you come back to every time you need to remember your power. You can return to these words, these traits, these reminders whenever life shakes you, whenever your old patterns creep back in.

Your Lower Self will show up, especially when you're making changes. That's normal. You've been thinking certain thoughts for too long, doing things in a certain way for too long. Your mind and your body are used to those patterns. So be patient. Change doesn't happen overnight—but it does happen when you choose it again and again.

Every time you're in a situation, pause and ask yourself:

Am I reacting from my Lower Self or responding from my Higher Self? Are these thoughts coming from fear, doubt, or lack—or from love, faith, and abundance?

The power lies in that moment of choice.
When you're overthinking, doubting your manifestations, victimizing yourself, making excuses, or lacking the discipline to do what needs to be done—catch it.
That's your Lower Self trying to take over again.
And in that moment, you gently remind yourself:
I can choose differently.

Your Higher Self is always connected—to the Universe, to God, to truth, to your intuition. That version of you knows what to do. I can't tell you how to handle every specific situation in this book, but if you pause and align with your Higher Self, the answer will always come.

Sometimes your Higher Self will tell you to trust the unknown.
Sometimes it's about letting go.
Sometimes it means putting the ego aside.
Sometimes it means stopping the spiral of thoughts, being still, being present.
Sometimes it's about taking bold, aligned action—not from lack or fear, but from trust and truth.

You won't always get it perfect. You'll react sometimes. You'll fall into old habits. That's part of being human. But your power is in recognizing it and realigning. And for me, what helps the most is this: I picture both my Higher Self and Lower Self standing in front of me. And I ask, *Which direction do I want to choose?*

Because no matter how difficult the moment is, you always have a choice.

This practice has transformed my life. I've been on this path for years, and it has helped me build better relationships with myself and others. I now attract friendships that match my frequency. I have more peace. I respond more and react less. I take actions from abundance instead of lack. I've created more opportunities, more joy, more alignment—just by choosing my Higher Self again and again.
And you can too.

There is always light in the tunnel. Even in the darkest seasons of life, your Higher Self will help you see it. You could take two people going through the exact same situation—one chooses to respond from their Higher Self, and the other reacts from their Lower Self. Their experiences will feel completely different. That's how powerful your perception and choices are.

So, nourish yourself—mind, body, soul. Eat well, move your body, rest.

Even if life feels overwhelming, take time each day—even if it's just 10 minutes—to be with yourself. That's self-love. And I don't mean just a face mask or a bath. I mean saying no when needed. Having boundaries. Trusting yourself. Respecting your own energy.
That is real self-love.

When I prioritized my relationship with myself, everything else improved. And yes, sometimes it might seem selfish. But in the spiritual world, filling your own cup first is essential. Because when your cup is full, you make better decisions, you show up better, you give more, and you create from a space of wholeness.

Now let's talk about manifesting.
Your dreams—whatever they are—require certainty. Whether it's peace of mind, deep love, success, freedom, or joy—manifestation doesn't just come from wishing. It comes from becoming. And becoming means aligning with your Higher Self.

If you have doubts, your manifestation delays. So sit with yourself. Meditate. Pray with faith, not desperation. Trust the dream in your heart, even if it feels too big or impossible. That dream was planted in you by the Universe—and that means it can happen.

Sometimes you'll need to take action. Sometimes you'll need to let go. Sometimes you'll need to trust with all your heart when there's no evidence yet. But every time you come back to your Higher Self, you're getting closer.
You're aligning. You're creating.

Before we close this book, I want to leave you with something that has deeply impacted my own journey—the Higher and Lower Self Challenge.

This is a practice I've been doing for years, and it has played a powerful role in helping me transform into the highest version of myself. It's supported me in building new habits, manifesting my desires, responding with more calm and clarity, and letting go of the patterns that once held me back.

Of course, this isn't something that happens overnight. It's a daily practice —a conscious choice to become more aware of who you're being and how you're showing up. Through this challenge, I invite you to choose one Higher Self trait you want to embody and one Lower Self trait you're ready to release. Commit to this for the next two or three weeks. Let it guide you. Let it ground you. Let it show you how powerful you really are when you live with intention.

A Final Reminder Before the Challenge

Before I guide you into the Higher and Lower Self challenge, I want to leave you with a few powerful reminders—because the truth is, manifesting your dreams isn't just about wishing. It's about aligning, acting, and choosing your Higher Self daily.

This work—this book—is one of the many tools that can help you connect to your Higher Self. It's a reminder that you always have the power to choose light over fear, love over doubt, and growth over stagnation.

But one thing you absolutely must do is take action.
If the version of you reading this right now isn't feeling fulfilled, isn't at peace, or isn't manifesting the life you desire—then that's your sign: there is work to do. And that's not a bad thing. That's a beautiful thing. It means you still have room to rise. You still have new versions of you to meet, become, and embody.

But transformation doesn't happen through hope alone. It happens through **discipline.** Through **consistency.** Through conscious, daily practice—not just physically, but mentally and emotionally.

If you want to change your thoughts, you must act on them every day.
If you want to build new beliefs, you must reinforce them consistently.
If you want more confidence, you have to practice being that version of you—even when it feels uncomfortable.

Change takes time. You've spent years thinking, reacting, and living one way—so give yourself at least a few weeks of discipline and devotion to shift into something new. Make it your priority. Because when you upgrade yourself month by month, thought by thought, habit by habit—you begin to attract your desires naturally. You don't need to force anything. You simply align with it.

And when you align, you shift realities.

I know this because I've lived it.
I've transformed myself over and over again. I didn't become who I am by accident—it took years of practice, deep self-work, and spiritual growth. I started this path when I was very young, carrying many insecurities, wounds, and inner battles. But what kept me going were the reminders I gave myself daily, the goals I set with unwavering faith, and the deep respect I had for the life I knew I deserved.

There was no "plan B" for me. I didn't allow excuses. And if I ever caught myself making one, I corrected it immediately. That's the kind of commitment you must bring to the version of you that's waiting to rise.

So please—be consistent. Be disciplined. Be patient.
Even if you fail at first, keep going. I did too. And in the beginning, I was harsh with myself—but even that I had to unlearn. Now I choose compassion.

Be kind. Speak to yourself like a queen. Give yourself time.
Because changing thoughts, habits, and beliefs is no small task—it's a rebirth. And like any rebirth, it requires tenderness, strength, and time.

But if you commit to it, if you choose yourself fully—your manifestations will become effortless.

And now, let's begin the challenge.

The Higher and Lower Self Challenge

This challenge has the power to transform your life. It's your invitation to shift whatever needs to change—starting now.

Here's how it works:
Choose any Lower Self trait from this book that you know you're still holding onto. It could be a pattern, belief, or emotional reaction that no longer serves you. Write it down. Get clear on what you want to shift.

Now choose the Higher Self trait that can replace it.
This becomes your daily challenge: to live, act, and respond as that version of you for the next 2 to 3 weeks.

Every day, remind yourself:

- Who am I choosing to be today?
- What thought, habit, or belief am I shifting?
- What does my Higher Self do in this moment?

When your Lower Self shows up, pause. Breathe.
Remind yourself gently but firmly: ***I don't live there anymore.***

When your Higher Self is needed, **lean into it. Embody it. Lead with it.**

Use tools that work for you:

- Set daily reminders on your phone with affirmations or mantras.
- Journal your experiences and patterns.
- Visualize both versions of you—see them clearly.
- Put your emotions aside just for a moment, and ask yourself: *Which version do I choose today?*

This visualization method helped me immensely. When I could see both versions in front of me—one rooted in fear and limitation, the other in love and power—I always knew which one I wanted to become. And so will you.

Because your Lower Self is not where your peace lives.

It's not where your dreams are born.

Your Higher Self is the version of you that creates magic.

A Reminder for the Journey

Sometimes it takes 21 days to shift a pattern. Sometimes it takes a month —or even longer. That doesn't matter.

What matters is that you keep going.

That you keep showing up.

That you keep choosing your Higher Self—even when you fall.

And yes—you will fall. I've failed more times than I can count. And every single time, I got up again. That's the journey.

Especially when you're shifting deep-rooted beliefs or lifelong thoughts, give yourself grace. These are not surface-level changes. These are rewrites of your entire inner story.

So be gentle.

Be kind.

And be patient with yourself.

Your timeline is your own. Don't compare it to anyone else's. We all come from different lives, different wounds, different families and beliefs. Honor your pace.

Some traits will come naturally to you. Others will take time. That's okay.

What matters is that you never give up on yourself.

I've been doing this work for years. And even now, there are traits I revisit and relearn. The deeper the root, the more love and patience it needs.

So from this moment on—no matter how long it takes—choose to become the best version of your Self.

A Note From My Heart

As we come to the end of this journey together, I want to thank you from the bottom of my heart for showing up—for yourself, and for your growth.

Everything is possible for you.
You can manifest anything you desire.
You can become anyone you choose to be.

Listen to your heart.
Trust your soul.
Follow your intuition, and the quiet guidance of the Creator.

When you stay true to your path and take the steps that feel aligned, doors will open—ones you never imagined possible.

Transformation takes time. It takes reminders.
So return to this book whenever you need clarity, strength, or a compass back to your power.

I believe in you. I always will.

With all my love,
Melanie

✦ The Lower Self Traits I Want to Let Go Of

In this space, write down the specific patterns, thoughts, reactions, or beliefs that you recognize as your Lower Self. These may be traits you've seen in yourself throughout this book — the ones you're now ready to outgrow. Be honest. Be gentle. This is your space for truth and release.

I am choosing to let go of:

✦ The Higher Self Traits I Want to Embody

Now, list the traits you want to fully step into — the ones that feel aligned with who you're becoming. Choose the qualities that inspire you, that feel like home, that match the version of you you're ready to live as. These are the energies you're calling in.

I am choosing to become:

Whispers from the Higher Self

You already are everything you seek to become.

The real you is not afraid — only the old you is.

Let go. If it's meant for you, it will return lighter, softer, better.

Discomfort is not the end — it's the beginning of transformation.

You don't need to force anything that flows with your soul.

You're not behind. You're being prepared.

Abundance begins when you stop acting from fear.

Your Higher Self doesn't rush. It knows the timing is divine.

Your peace is sacred. Protect it like your future depends on it — because it does.

Every time you choose the Higher Self, you rewrite your story.

Notes

Notes

Notes

Notes

Notes

Notes

Notes

Notes

Notes

Notes

Notes

www.ingramcontent.com/pod-product-compliance
Lightning Source LLC
LaVergne TN
LVHW060426210126
830229LV00025B/525